Solomon Caesar Malan

On Ritualism

Solomon Caesar Malan

On Ritualism

ISBN/EAN: 9783337336776

Printed in Europe, USA, Canada, Australia, Japan

Cover: Foto ©Lupo / pixelio.de

More available books at **www.hansebooks.com**

ON
RITUALISM.

BY THE

REV. S. C. MALAN, M.A.,
OF BALLIOL COLLEGE, OXFORD; AND VICAR OF BROADWINDSOR.

LONDON:
SAUNDERS, OTLEY, AND CO.,
66, BROOK STREET, W.

MDCCCLXVII.

[*All Rights Reserved.*]

LONDON:
WILLIAM STEVENS, PRINTER, 37, BELL YARD,
TEMPLE BAR.

CONTENTS.

	Page
I.—THE "CATHOLIC REVIVAL"	1
II.—OF CATHOLIC VESTMENTS	20
III.—OF THE ENGLISH CHURCH, OF THE RE-UNION OF CHRISTENDOM, AND OF THE HOLY EUCHARIST	42
IV.—OF INCENSE, OF LIGHTS, AND OF THE EUCHARISTIC SACRIFICE	75
V.—OF THE PRIESTHOOD, AND OF THE VESTMENTS THEREOF	101

PREFACE.

HAD I been aware that these articles on Ritualism should ever be reprinted, I would have bestowed on them greater care than I did, when thinking them intended only for the ephemeral columns of a newspaper. As it is, however, I had no idea they were to re-appear in this form, until I received the first four sheets for correction; so that I have not had an opportunity of treating the whole subject as I should have done, both more fully and in better order; even though in the opinion of Ritualists, "theologians like me, be among the worst enemies the Church has to contend with."

—Fancy my confessing to such judges!—But my MASTER is theirs also.

Such as I be, then, the following pages were nevertheless written with honest and sincere love for the Church to which, by the grace of GOD, I belong. Thirty years in her Holy Orders, added to a certain acquaintance with Fathers and divines of more than one or two countries, and, withal, a very varied experience of what the "Holy Catholic and Apostolic Church" is in general, and what the Roman section of it is in particular, enable me, without consulting others, to form my own judgment both of what is or should be Anglican and Catholic, and of what is nothing but Popery. So that, not only can I draw the distinction between what would be an Anglican Revival, and what may, perhaps, in the end, turn out to be more like Rome stirring up the embers of Ridley, Cranmer, and of their fellows, though, for the present, it be with the crosier, instead of the sword—but, also, shall I not easily be persuaded, against the evidence of my own senses, that this ado about "Cathol-

Preface. vii

icism" embraces in the mind of those who make it much more of "the Church Catholic" than Rome and Romanism. And, as the more they resent this the more true it is, they had better at once acquiesce in it.

No doubt that, in this Ritualistic excitement —or, I should rather say, bewilderment—since we are told that "Catholicism in England, after having been moored 300 years, now finds itself at sea, signalising for a pilot to steer it safe amid the breakers of lace, incense, and satins;" for some Bona to settle the "Catholic" posture in bowing, and the riteful number of noddings and mutterings; the standard length and colour of stoles and chasubles, of copes and maniples, and the weight and matter of tapers and taper-sticks —there are men good and pious. But, as they must appear, withal, weak and silly, if they can busy themselves or even quarrel about such things at a time when the Church and the State require all the prayers, all the wisdom, and the most matured judgment men can bring to bear on them, and while millions of their fellow men at their own doors are dying in ignorance of "righteousness, temperance, and judgment to come"—one cannot but think there are also among them a good many men, neither pious, weak, nor silly—but designing.

For when, on the one hand, we see the utter disregard shown by Ritualists for the episcopal authority to which they pledged themselves to obey, setting at naught everything but their own will and whims, and, withal, splitting among themselves on the most futile questions, being it appears not only at sea, but, it would seem, also in a fog, without chart, compass, or timekeeper, going hither and thither, first using one ritual, then another, then a mixture of both, then neither the one nor the other—no man that is not either foolish or misled by others can help drawing from it the inference that if those men owe allegiance to any one, it is not, assuredly, to their Bishops and to the Church they still affect to call their own; but that this *Divide et impera*, simple cause and effect, originates in Romanism: by what name soever it may suit the Ritualists to

Preface.

call it. Since, in the name of common sense, what are we to think of a "Catholic ritual" that differs in the several churches of the same city in which it is said to be observed, or of a "Catholicism" on which a handful of men cannot agree?

On the other hand, were this movement honestly Anglican, whereby I mean kindled and fanned by men who, one could think, did frankly love their Church and nation, and without any Romish inklings; who had not only begun their work fairly by paying courteous deference to their respective Bishops, but also tried to strengthen their hands, and to encourage them in doing the work of keeping order and of spreading sound teaching and true religion among the people; men, in short, who, being "true Catholics," would think it doing GOD and the people better service to bring back to the Church even a few sheep gone astray than to scare many more from the fold by lengthening their stoles and trimming their maniples, and who would thus honestly and aboveboard help to cement with union, love, earnestness and unity the framework of the Commonwealth, and with it the stones of the Church that are loosened, and bid fair to crumble away—I, for my part, would join in it heart and soul. But, from the way it began, and from the spirit of defiance in which it is carried on, it is very plain that such arrogant independence in the priests will never teach humility to their flocks; that so bitter a root will never bring forth any fruit good for much; and that the whole thing is so un-English that it must be of foreign growth. I will, therefore, keep aloof from it. None of this "Ritualism" shall ever be seen in any of my three churches as long as I have the charge of them; for I think it more to the glory of GOD, and for the good of my parishioners, that these should be made Christians by being brought to church, taught and kept there, in the way to which they have been accustomed, or at least in a way that creates no offence, than that they should be scared from it into dissent by some crotchet of folly of my own.

As regards this Ritualism, then, and more,

perhaps, for what lies under than for what appears on the surface, I would, in the vulgar tongue, say, —*Timeo Danaos,* &c., but for the more elegant idiom of that shrewd mouse, to which Greek was not "weariness of the flesh," as it seems to be to some of the Ritualistic Clergy—ὦ οὗτος, κἂν θύλαξ γένῃ σύ, οὐ προσελευσόμεθά σοι, the moral of which is variously explained in most languages; but in Ethiopic, it reads, "A man once bitten by a snake is ware of a slip of willow-bark."

I may as well mention that I adopted the form of dialogue only as more convenient, and not in order to give both Ritualistic opinions and mine; except indeed, when I repeat expressions I have heard used by Ritualists. For, in sooth, if they have no better plea than what I put forth on their behalf, it is little enough.

S. C. MALAN.

Broadwindsor, March 6th, 1867.

I.—THE "CATHOLIC REVIVAL."

*ITUALIST.* You should have attended High Mass at S—— yesterday; the vestments worn there by the Clergy were splendid; it quite revived me to see them.

Catholic. "High Mass," do you say? Not for me. Besides, I was celebrating the Holy Communion in my own church, and could not have gone. I see you went to what you call a "Catholic Revival."

Ritualist. And what else would you call it?

Catholic. I? As a simple-minded, plain-spoken man, I should call it a Romish or Popish Revival, if it be a revival at all; if not, a Romish service, or something very much like it.

Ritualist. Well, but is not "Romish" the same as "Catholic"?

Catholic. May be you think so. For my part, I understand the term "Catholic" to mean "universal, everywhere the same;" in the sense in which

Justin Martyr speaks of καθολικὴ ἀνάστασις τῶν νεκρῶν καὶ κρίσις (Dial. c. Tryph. p. 308), "of the universal or general resurrection of the dead and of the universal judgment."

Ritualist. Well, *quod semper, quod ubique, quod*——

Catholic. Exactly, but not as you seem to take it. Thus, my idea of the Catholic Church is "the blessed company of all faithful people," as I am taught to call it, not only by the Church to which I belong (Post-Com. Serv. 2nd coll.), but also by other branches of the Church Catholic; as, for instance, by the Russian Church, that defines the Church Catholic to be "the whole assembly (or multitude) of believers—the Head of which is Christ" (Catech. Moscow, 1831, p. 52, *et seq.*); by the Armenian (Gregorian) Church, that says the Church consists of "all true Christians" (Catech. Constant. 1865, p. 27, Moscow, 1850, p. 50); by the Georgian Church, that styles it "a company instituted of GOD, wherein men are joined together by one common orthodox faith, and by an ordained Clergy and Sacraments—with One Head, the Lord Jesus Christ" (Catech. Tiflis, 1865, p. 88), wherein the confession of faith of the Armenian (Gregorian) Church agrees, when it says of the Church Catholic that "it consists in the assembly of all orthodox Christians who were baptised in the name of the Father and of the Son and of the Holy Ghost," adding, "and who confess the Faith of Christ according to the ancient Fathers" (Confess. of Faith, Arm. 1667, p. 22).

Also by the Greek Church, that calls the Catholic Church " an assembly of people, the Body of Christ, called the Spouse of Christ, cleansed by the water of baptism, and sprinkled with the Blood of Christ —whose pearls are the Divine teachings of our Saviour and of His disciples—whose Head is Christ Himself" (German. Patr. in Ἱερὰ κατήχ. περὶ τῆς Ἐκκλησ. p. 31). Likewise, πιστεύομεν τὴν λεγομένην καθολικὴν ἐκκλησίαν τοὺς ἐν Χριστῷ πιστοὺς καθόλου περιέχειν—" We believe," says Cyril Lucar. (Confess. Eccles. Or. cap. x.), "that the Church Catholic embraces in general (or wholly) the faithful in Christ." (So also, word for word, Synod. Hieros. 1672, under Patr. Dositheus, Decret. x.) Καθολικὴ μὲν οὖν καλεῖται διὰ τὸ κατὰ πάσης εἶναι τῆς οἰκουμένης, " the Church is said to be Catholic," says S. Cyril of Jerusalem (Catech. xviii.), " from her spreading all over the habitable world;" ἡ κατὰ τὴν οἰκουμένην καθολικὴ ἐκκλησία, " of which our Lord Jesus Christ, the Saviour of our souls, and the Ruler of our bodies, is, ποιμήν, Shepherd" (Martyr. Polyc. viii. xix). Since ὅπου ἂν ᾖ Χριστὸς Ἰησοῦς, ἐκεῖ ἡ καθολικὴ ἐκκλησία, "where Jesus Christ is, there is the Catholic Church," says S. Ignatius (ad Eph. viii).

The Catholic Church, then, is the assembly of those who believe in Christ, according to what the holy Apostle says: that "whosoever believeth that Jesus is the Christ is born of GOD" (1 S. John v. 1). This is "the faith which was once delivered unto the saints" (S. Jude 3), "which is always the same and always new," says S. Cyril of Alexandria (Ep. in Zoega Codd. Sahid. 278); "and that rests not on men's inventions," says S. Cyril of Jerusalem, "but is preserved whole only by proofs drawn from the Holy Scriptures;" ἐκ πάσης γραφῆς ὀχυρωμένη, "borne out and fortified as it is by the whole Scripture" (Catech. iv. & v.) Concerning this S. Ephraem speaks yet more positively, when he says (Adv. Hæres. Serm. xxii.) "that, as the alphabet is a whole, made up of letters from which not one is to be taken out, so also is the Truth contained in the letters of the Holy Gospel a full measure, from which nothing may be taken, neither more nor less." And this but agrees with S. Paul's words, that "faith cometh by hearing, and hearing by the Word of GOD" (Rom. x. 17). So that, this faith in Christ is alone the bond of the Catholic Church, being "the foundation than which none other can man lay" (1 Cor iii. 11), since it is declared by Christ Himself to be "the Rock upon which He would build His Church" (S. Matt. xvi. 18).

With this definition of the Catholic Church the Roman teaching stands in strange contrast, whether we take the Tridentine Confession of Faith—

"Sanctam Catholicam et Apostolicam Romanam Ecclesiam, omnium Ecclesiarum matrem, et magistram agnosco, Romanoque Pontifici, B. Petri Apostolorum principis successori, ac Jesu Christi vicario, veram obedientiam spondeo ac juro" Syllog. Confess. 5)

—or adopt the explanation given by Cardinal Bellarmine, in answer to the question, What means "the Church"? (Dottrina Crist. Roma. 1842, p. 54, *et seq.*):

"The Church means a *convocation* and a *congregation of men*, who are baptised, who make profession of the Faith and of the law of Christ in subjection to the sovereign Roman Pontiff. It is said to be a *convocation*, because we do not come into the world Christians, as we do Italians or French; but we enter into this congregation through baptism, which is, as it were, the door into the Church. But it is not enough to be baptised in order to be members of the Church; a man must believe and confess the holy Faith and the law of Christ, as they are taught by the pastors and preachers of the Church; yet is not even this enough; for a man must also submit himself to the Sovereign Pontiff of Rome as to the Vicar of Christ, that is, he must acknowledge and hold him for (*superiore* Supremo *in luogo di Cristo*) his supreme lord and master in the place of Christ."

This, at all events, is plain speaking; for a comment on which I may refer you to Dr. Barrow's treatise on the Pope's supremacy; while Hooker sums up both the one side and the other, saying (Eccl. Pol. bk. v. p. 471):—

"Because the *only object* which separateth ours from other religions is Jesus Christ, in whom none but the Church doth believe, and whom none but the Church doth worship, we find that accordingly the Apostles do everywhere distinguish hereby the Church from infidels and from Jews, accounting them which call upon the name of our Lord Jesus Christ to be His Church.

"If we go lower, we shall but add unto this certain casual and variable accidents, which are not properly of the being, but make only for the happier and better being of the Church of God, either in deed or in men's opinions and conceits. This is the error of all Popish definitions that hitherto have been brought. They define not the Church by that which the Church essentially is, but by that wherein they imagine their own more perfect than the rest are."

Yet this does no more than say, in language suited to our own times, what S. Clement of Alexandria already said in the second century, ὅτι γὰρ μεταγενεστέρας τῆς καθολικῆς ἐκκλησίας τὰς ἀνθρωπίνας συνηλύσεις πεποιήκασιν, οὐ πολλῶν δεῖ λόγων, namely, that "we need not be at the trouble to show that men's conventicles are of later date than the Church Catholic"—κατά τε ἀρχὴν, κατά τε ἐξοχὴν, μόνην εἶναι φαμὲν ἀρχαίαν καὶ καθολικὴν ἐκκλησίαν, εἰς ἑνότητα πίστεως μιᾶς—" But, both as regards origin and as regards excellence, we call that Church alone primitive and Catholic which, by the counsel of the One GOD, and through the One Lord, brings together into the unity of one Faith, that rests on her own testaments, or, rather, on the testament which is one and the same during different times, those whom GOD had ordained and predestinated; knowing as He did before the foundation of the world, that they would be righteous" (Stromat. lib. vii. p. 764, *et seq.*). Although here S. Clement evidently embraces the whole of Christ's Church, both visible and invisible, under the term "Catholic" or universal, yet his meaning is plain as regards the visible Church on earth, to which alone we now allude. In the words of Lactantius (Divin. Inst. lib. iv. c. xxx.): "Sola igitur Catholica Ecclesia est, quæ verum cultum retinet."

Ritualist. Very good; but in the course of time, you see——

Catholic. I know, the enemy sowed tares; and master-builders of various sorts built upon the foundation, some with gold and silver, and many others also with wood, hay, and stubble. Since, therefore, a portion of the building of the Christian Church on earth is made up of stones that will last, while another portion is reared with materials that will be destroyed, although they rest on the foundation, you see yourself clearly, that no one part of the human superstructure can be called " Catholic, general, or universal ;" and that, strictly speaking, no other part of the Church deserves that name than the foundation, which is THE FAITH IN CHRIST in which alone all Christians agree. Whence it follows (1) that a Church can call itself a part of the Catholic Church, τῆς καθολικῆς ἐκκλησίας παροικία (Martyr. Polyc. Inscr.), only in so far as it rests on the foundation and is one with it; (2) that the only "Catholic" element in all the several branches of the Church Catholic consists in the point or points upon which all those several branches are, for the time being, agreed; (3) that everything else in them may be national, popular, local, individual, or peculiar, but is not "Catholic," since it is not common to all; and (4) that none of these branches of the Church can call its own peculiarities "Catholic" except through overweening assumption and ignorance.

Therefore, ere you can call the present religious excitement in a small portion of the Church of England a "Catholic revival," must you, like a sensible man, first show that it is "a revival" at all; that is, a throb of real Christian and spiritual life; and, secondly, that it is a revival of faith, doctrine, vestments, postures, and ceremonies, which, at any time since the foundation of the Christian Church, were universally held and adopted by that Church. Failing this, they can at best be but the revival of such doctrines, vestments, postures, and ceremonies as are either identical with those of some other section of the Church, or akin to them, but are not "Catholic."

However, not only shall you find some difficulty in thus proving them to be "Catholic," but, ere you try, it may save you trouble to know that you never will succeed, inasmuch as at no time were they Catholic; that is, generally received in the Church. But, may be, you will find they come to you straight through the Romish Church, which is, of course, only one branch of the Christian Church, and is, so far from being itself "the Catholic Church," whatever be the arrogant assumption with which it claims that title, that, as you doubtless know perfectly well, it is simply hated, if not in many points anathematised, by that far larger and more ancient portion of the Church Catholic which alone calls itself "orthodox." Ὁ Δίκερως Γίγας τῆς Ῥώμης, ὁ Πάπας φημί· ὁ ὁποῖος κοντὰ ὅπου εἶναι ἐσωτερικὸς καὶ κατὰ πνεῦμα ἀρχιερεὺς, θέλει νὰ εἶναι ἐξωτερικὸς καὶ κατὰ σῶμα βασιλεύς· νὰ εὐλογῇ καὶ νὰ θανατοῖ, νὰ κρατῇ τὴν ποιμαντικὴν βακτηρίαν, καὶ μάχαιραν τὴν φονευτρίαν. Μίξις ἄμικτος, καὶ τέρας ἀλλόκοτον. κ.τ.λ. "I speak," says the Greek priest, "of that Gigas Bicornis, the Pope of Rome, who, while being of the inner world and High Priest in the Spirit, wishes also to belong to the outer world and to be king in the body; to bless and to kill; to hold the pastoral staff, and to wield the sword in order to smite with it. Unheard of confusion and hideous monstrosity!" etc. (ἑρμην. τοῦ πγ΄. καν. τῶν ἁγ. ἀπ. p. 61. See also Council Laodic. p. 259, 260, and sixth Council *ibid.*, p. 121, etc., published by authority of the Holy Synod of Athens, 1841). Such amenities are but faint murmurs from the gulf that yawns between the Eastern Church and that of Rome, and which A. P. U. C. will have to bridge over or to fill up ere their day-dream of the re-union of Christendom can come to pass before the time appointed for it.

Ritualist. But surely, setting aside the question of what is, and of what is not, Catholic, do you not think that a certain outward show in Divine service is not only allowable, but necessary?

Catholic. I do, most assuredly; but this is another question. We were speaking of the Church

Catholic, and we saw that, of that Church, the foundation alone, laid by our Lord Himself, can properly be called "Catholic," and that all the rest of the superstructure is more or less human, and therefore partakes more or less of the human will and infirmities.

Ritualist. What, then, do you call the Church?

Catholic. The Church is Apostolic as well as Catholic; as the Abyssinian Church quaintly defines it, "the House of Christians that consists of every congregation that is of the Apostles," having been founded by them among all nations, whither they went in obedience to this command of their Master, "Go ye, and teach all nations, baptising them in the name of the Father, and of the Son, and of the Holy Ghost: teaching them to observe all things whatsoever I have commanded you" (S. Matt. xxviii. 19, 20). This shows that the Apostles received not only their mission, but also the very doctrine they were to teach; and which was to be brought to their remembrance by the Spirit which their Master would send over them, and through which He promised "to be with them unto the end of the world."

Ritualist. Well, but this would not prevent them from ordering certain things, as occasion required, and which are not left on record, but may have been handed down through tradition.

Catholic. Quite so: thus Titus was left by S. Paul in Crete that "he should set in order the things that were wanting." But, inasmuch as, even in this case, Titus and the Apostle "walked in the same steps, and had the same Spirit" that reminded, and taught, and guided the other Apostles during their mission, the result should be everywhere the same, and those traditions, supposing they did exist, should agree in all points, since there could be no contradiction in the promptings of the self-same Spirit.

Such, however, is not the case. We have no "Catholic," that is, no universal, traditions that we can trace to the Apostles. On the other hand, we find that, for all things necessary to the constitution and to the welfare of the Churches they planted, they left distinct precepts on record in their Acts and in their Epistles. We find that they administered the two Sacraments that were, the one used and consecrated, the other instituted by Christ; and that they ordained and appointed a clergy, consisting of Bishops, Priests, and Deacons, to minister to the laity some of the gifts they inherited from the Apostles. Whence we see (1) that the Church became Catholic in faith and spirit, at the same time that she was Apostolic in form; since the Apostles founded her by teaching that Faith and imparting those gifts; (2) that, considering the teaching they received from Christ and through His Spirit, and their charge to the Bishops they ordained, "to hold fast the form of sound words they had received from them" (2 Tim. i. 13, etc.), being so fully persuaded of their own Divine commission as to judge them accursed that should preach another gospel than the one they taught (Gal. i. 8, 9), we may conclude (3) not only that their writings are our only real authority for what is both Catholic and Apostolic, but also that no Church can call itself both "Catholic and Apostolic" that does not hold the Faith, does not administer the Sacraments, and does not ordain the threefold ministry of Bishops, Priests, and Deacons instituted by the Apostles. Of course it is not for either you or me to limit the grace of GOD to one particular outward form of Church; and good men may be found in all forms thereof. Nevertheless, as those forms differ one from another, we may deem that the best, the most Catholic and most Apostolic, that comes nearest the pattern left us by the Apostles, with the smallest proportion of human devices added to their teaching; besides which teaching nothing can be binding on us as an article of "Catholic and Apostolic" faith. So that, supposing you and I agreed on other points, I would also join with you in this matter of vestments, that seem of such importance in your eyes, if you could prove to me (1) that they are "Catholic;" that is, in use wherever the Catholic Faith "that Jesus is the Christ" prevails, and (2) that they are "Apostolic;" that they were first worn by the Apostles and then came down to us from them.

Do you, then, believe that these vestments, with

the genuflexions, postures, and ceremonies of this so-called "Catholic revival," are "Catholic;" I mean, exactly of the same form and meaning in the Romish, the Greek, the Russian, the Georgian, the Armenian, the Syrian, Maronite, Jacobite, and Nestorian, the Coptic, the Abyssinian, and other Churches?

Ritualist. I dare say not.

Catholic. You are right, as you shall see by-and-by. Do you then believe they are "Apostolic;" either that our Lord Himself wore something like them at the Last Supper, or that the Apostles put them on when ministering either at Troas or in the house of Nymphas at Colossæ?

Ritualist. I could not say they did.

Catholic. Here, again, you are honest; for your own authorities, "after showing plainly that the heads of the Church and the other ministers of the altar wore, at the celebration of the Holy Mysteries, a dress of the same shape as that worn by the laity of the Roman Empire," go on to say, " Hence arises the question—Did the Apostles and their successors also, during the first three centuries, administer the Sacraments in their every-day dress, or did they, when able, put on other vestments? Some men hold one view, and others another." As of course they must; for who is to decide since "quales autem hi ritus fuerint, quos ipsa consecravit Apostolorum auctoritas, ob veterum monumentorum inopiam, quis pro certo definiet?"

says truly the same author, who, therefore, adds candidly: "Fatemur quidem Apostolos, eorumque primos successores ubi illud exegerint temporum angustiæ, aut alia necessitas, in *communi* eorum et *vulgari* veste sacram peregisse Liturgiam"—We are bound to admit that the Apostles, as well as their immediate successors, whether owing to the straitness of the times or to some other necessity, did perform the Sacred Liturgy in their common everyday dress. (Augustini Krazer De Liturgiis Apostolicis, etc., liber singul. 1786, p. 261, § 2, 3.)

Ritualist. But did not S. Paul write to Timothy about the cloak he had left with Carpus at Troas?

Catholic. He did; if, indeed, the φαιλόνη be not, as some think, the case that contained his books and parchments. Be it a cloak, however; what of that? You might as well affirm that the books of which he also wrote were "early editions," or that his parchments were the plays of Sophocles, as with certain men to say "You have no doubt" that cloak was the robe S. Paul wore in his ministrations; a very bold assertion, you must own.

But, besides the cloak of S. Paul, there is also "si omnimodà possit adhiberi fides," if one could only believe it anyhow, says the learned Augustine, "*vestis sacerdotalis* Johannis Evangelistæ," the sacerdotal robes of S. John the Evangelist, handed down to Gregory the Great, of which Joa.

Diaconus speaks, "and *Planeta Sacra* Petri Apostoli," the consecrated chasuble of Peter the Apostle, brought from Antioch to Paris, as Hugo Monachus affirms; and, again, " *Sacra Tunica* S. Jacobi," the consecrated tunic or albe of S. James, mentioned in the Acts of S. Sylvester ; " si, inquam, ejusmodi historiis omnimodâ posset adhiberi fides, res esset confecta," if, only, as I say, one could anyhow believe all this, the thing would be settled. So it would, no doubt. " Ast rident ejusmodi historias moderni critici," but modern critics laugh at such stories ; and no wonder, since they are too much even for a Cardinal, as the good Augustine says in despair: " nec magnam illis fidem adhibet ipse Card. Bona," even Card. Bona does not think much of them, whether from the remote antiquity in question, or from the complete silence of all ancient writers on the subject. The author of the Ἱερὰ κατήχησις (p. 23), a work for the Greek Clergy, published by authority, tells the same stories, omitting, however, S. James's tunic. But both authors seem ignorant of our Saviour's coat, said to be preserved in the ancient Cathedral of Mtzkhsetha, and worshipped there as a relic.

Ritualist. Yet the Bishops and the Clergy of the early Church must have worn some distinctive dress, at least during the Liturgy.

Catholic. Possibly ; but what ? You see your own authorities cannot tell. Had we the well-authenticated pattern of only one vestment worn by the Apostles, or by their immediate successors, that, I grant you, would be a sufficient guide for us to follow. But we have nothing whatever of the sort. The Apostles not only never call themselves "priests," ἱερεῖς, in the sense of "sacerdos," but they must have thought, either that the matter of vestments was of no moment, or that the spiritual service and the spiritual priesthood they established, in the place of the Levitical types under the law, could borrow nothing from that— no more, in short, than light borrows from a shadow, the day from the night, or the fulfilment of a prophecy from the prophecy itself. Were these vestments and gestures now talked of, necessary for the life of the Catholic and Apostolic Church, the Apostles, who laid rules of faith, gave precepts of order in so many things, would assuredly not have overlooked the matter of priestly and of pontifical attire. Whereas not only are they themselves silent on the subject, but there is no allusion to it in their so-called Canons, that are of the highest authority in the Greek Church; neither can I find any clue to the shape or to the colour of priestly garments, properly so called, in the writings of the Apostolic Fathers, nor yet in those of their immediate successors.

For instance, Justin Martyr, who speaks in detail of the Lord's Supper and of the manner in which it was administered, does not give us to understand that it was then done with greater pomp than when the Apostles "brake bread from house to house," when he speaks of the bread, water, and wine being brought τῷ προεστῶτι τῶν ἀδελφῶν, "to the president of the brethren," to be consecrated by him, and to be distributed to the faithful alone, εὐχαριστήσαντος τοῦ προεστῶτος, "after the president had blessed those elements and had given thanks" (Pro Christ. Apol. ii. p. 97). Even three hundred years after, when the Church had already departed from her first simplicity, and S. Cyril of Jerusalem, speaking of the Holy Eucharist (Catech. Mystag. v.) as being celebrated no longer by τὸν προεστῶτα τῶν ἀδελφῶν, but now by τὸν ἱερέα καὶ τοὺς κυκλόντας τὸ θυσιαστήριον πρεσβυτέρους, "by the priest celebrant and the presbyters around the altar," he says nothing either in this or in any other place concerning the vestments worn by those priests. But I mention him only by the way; for in a matter of this kind, that should be both a Catholic and an Apostolic institution, in order to deserve the importance some men attach to it, I should think it hardly fair to inquire into authorities later than the first or the second century; since the Church Catholic dates from before that time.

Ritualist. But surely the Church has power both to order rites and ceremonies and to suppress them if necessary; and likewise vestments, of course.

Catholic. No doubt, but this, you see, does not make them "Catholic," unless they be universally adopted, nor "Apostolic," if later than the Apostolic times.

Ritualist. I see, you are a " Bible Christian."

Catholic. If you mean by this that I believe " Holy Scripture containeth all things necessary to salvation; so that whatsoever is not read therein, nor may be proved thereby, is not to be required of any man that it should be believed as an article of faith, or be thought requisite or necessary to salvation"—I do hold this to be true and truly to be the teaching of the Fathers, which I once subscribed, as you also did at your ordination; and in this I agree with the host of Christ's holy confessors and martyrs, who, like Archbishop Laud, held that "the belief of Scripture to be the Word of GOD and infallible, is an equal, or, rather, a preceding, prime principle of faith, with or to the whole body of the Creed" (Relat. of Confer. p. 27, 28). In matters, however, which are purely of rule or government, I bow first to the authority of the Church Catholic, and then to that of my own Church. In the matter even of vestments and of ceremonies, therefore, that are wholly of human invention, and altogether arbitrary and optional, and, as Hooker says, "indifferent," I should with him also "judge it even at the first an impudent thing for a man bred and brought up in the Church to be of a contrary mind without a cause." For in this case, nothing but the authority of the whole Catholic Church could override that of a single branch of it. We see, however, that these vestments and these ceremonies cannot honestly be called either Catholic or Apostolic; they must, therefore, be more or less peculiar; they are not exactly Greek—whence then, do they come?

Ritualist. But you have no better authority for your surplice. Do you imagine that the Apostles, S. Ignatius, or S. Polycarp, wore one?

Catholic. Not one exactly like mine, perhaps; but that they wore a garment of the same colour is hardly to be questioned, as we shall see by-and-by, when we speak of the symbolism of your vestments. At all events, the voice of the primitive Church is only in favour of a white priestly garment, all coloured ones being later innovations. But of this when we meet again. For the present, let it suffice to have shown that, if you wish to speak correctly, you cannot say of the present excitement, innovations, or so-called revival, that it is "Catholic."

II.—OF CATHOLIC VESTMENTS.

Catholic. We saw that your "revival" is not "Catholic"; now what about your vestments?

Ritualist. Setting aside for the present the question of their being or not Catholic or Apostolic, I must own, I like the pomp, the glitter, and the outward show of them. Surely you cannot object to something of the sort; only think of the splendour of GOD'S service in the Temple at Jerusalem. I wonder you are not tired of your monotonous surplice, stole, hood, and gown; for my part, I am; I must, therefore, seek consolation in something else.

Catholic. I am sorry to find your faith is so weak and your devotion so faint as to require such aids. With you I deprecate the coldness, the carelessness, and even the slovenliness often shown by certain clergymen in the performance of GOD'S service in His house; and with you, also, I have no opinion of the public state of religion that can leave that

II.—Of Catholic Vestments.

House in a dilapidated state. I also grant you, as a matter of course, that, in sincere men, outward demonstration is but the expression of their inward piety and earnestness; and that, in their private devotions at home, they may adopt what form they please. But you and I would differ as to the nature and as to the amount of display required in our public service of GOD; seeing that our Christian worship, which is to be "in spirit and in truth," can borrow little or nothing from the Jewish ritual that was one (1) of pomp, as unto Him who was both GOD and King of the nation, and also (2) one of shadows of spiritual realities in which we live. Therefore, as regards the outward form of public worship, which every branch of the Catholic Church has full right to choose for herself, it must of necessity not only depend on good taste, but on the national character of the people; such things being mere externals concerning which neither our Lord nor His Apostles have left us any pattern or directions; things, therefore, that should be framed according to that national taste and character, and be suited thereto in order to promote edification. "That which inwardly each man should be," says Hooker (bk. v. ch. vi. 2), "the Church outwardly ought to testify. And, therefore, the duties of our religion which are seen must be such as that affection which is unseen ought to be. Signs must resemble the things they signify. If religion bear the greatest sway in our hearts, our outward religious duties must show it as far as the Church hath outward ability. Duties of religion, performed by whole societies of men, ought to have in them, according to our power, a sensible excellency, correspondent to the majesty of Him whom we worship. Yea, then are the public duties of religion best ordered when the Militant Church doth resemble by sensible means, as it may in such cases, that hidden dignity and glory wherewith the Church triumphant in heaven is beautified."

Ritualist. There; that is just what I said. You see that Hooker agrees with me.

Catholic. He wrote this in answer to the Puritans, who railed against even the use of the surplice, as being Popish, and which you dislike as being Anglican; wherein both you and they show either prejudice or ignorance. "Let our first demand be therefore," says the same wise man, "that in the external form of religion such things as are apparently, or can be sufficiently proved, effectual and generally fit to set forward godliness, either as betokening the greatness of GOD, or as beseeming the dignity of religion, or as concurring with celestial impressions in the minds of men, may be reverently thought of; some few, rare, casual, and tolerable, or otherwise curable, inconveniences notwithstanding" (*ibid.* p. 38). So that, since your present ritualistic practices are a complete and sudden innovation upon that which the sober taste and the good sense of the nation have established by common consent ever since the Reformation—that is, for about three hundred years—unless you be prepared to incur the blame of being injudicious, reckless, may be, personally vain and willing rather to sacrifice the greater good of the many to the lesser good of the few, or to some fancies and crotchets of your own, you must first—and since these practices are not "Catholic"—show proof that they are (1) signs resembling that which they signify; (2) the necessary outward expression of inward worship; (3) that the worship cannot be performed adequately and worthily without them; (4) that they are, therefore, "effectual and generally fit to set forward godliness;" and (5) that the public worship of GOD, as at present ordered and appointed, when duly performed in the English Church, is insufficient to promote godliness, and is, therefore, to be not only modified and rectified, but even remodelled after your own pattern, at all costs, even at that of creating offence and scandal in the Church. And, therefore, (6) that so urgent is the case as to justify you, who profess to correct what is amiss, and to teach obedience and humility, to act in defiance of your Bishop's advice and authority, and of the opinion of the more sober-minded men in the Church.

Ritualist. The Bishops say nothing; and as to the opinion of the Clergy, the Report of Convocation on Ritual left us free to do as we like.

Catholic. That Report always struck me as a rather weak production; as if the men engaged in it were either unwilling or afraid, or, perhaps, did not know how to grapple with the subject. And as to the conduct of the Bishops in this matter, all I can say is that I do not understand it. Some of them speak plain enough, yet, as a body, they look to me as if they were not agreed among themselves, forgetting that, however much or little they may differ in their personal convictions, they should, at all events, agree together in the defence of their Church. But, since you seem to set up the tribunal of your own-self over and above all others—at least, in the Church of England—look at the question of change from the present customs three centuries old on its own merits.

"That which wisdom did first begin," quoth Hooker (bk. v., vii. 3), "and hath been with good men long continued, challengeth allowance of them that succeed, although it plead for itself nothing. That which is new"—and your ritualistic practices are new, at the present time, in this country, say what you will of their antiquity—"if it promise not much, doth fear condemnation before trial ; till trial no man doth acquit or trust it, what good soever it pretend and promise. So that, in this kind, there are few things known to be good till such time as they grow to be ancient." "In which consideration there is cause why we should be slow and unwilling to change, without very urgent necessity, the ancient ordinances, rites, and long approved customs of our venerable predecessors." " Further, if it be a law which the custom and continual practice of many ages or years hath confirmed in the minds of men, to alter it must needs be troublesome and scandalous. It amazeth them; it causeth them to stand in doubt whether anything be in itself by nature either good or evil, and not all things rather such as men at this or that time agree to account of them, when they behold even those things disproved, disannulled, rejected, which use had made in a manner natural." "But as for arbitrary alterations, when laws in themselves not simply bad or unmeet, are changed for better and more expedient; if the benefit of that which is newly better devised be but small, sith the custom of easiness to alter and change is so evil, no doubt but to bear a tolerable sore is better than to venture on a dangerous remedy" (*ibid.*, bk. iv., xiv. 1, 2).

Ritualist. Still I do not see why I am not at liberty to adopt what vestments and what ceremonies I like.

Catholic. In private you may do what you please; but, as your public ministration is not your own, but the property of the Church, which, for this reason, not only placed you under rule and authority, in order thereby to secure union and uniformity, and to guard against the confusion and disorder that would inevitably result from an arbitrary freedom of action granted to every clergyman, but also pays you to maintain that order, you cannot take upon yourself alone, apart from the Church's leave and authority, through her Bishops in Synod assembled, and, in England, with the sanction of the State, to bring in any change or material innovation, without incurring the charge (1) of assuming what does not belong to you, with greater audacity, if not effrontery, than befits you as priest in the Church Catholic. And (2) of not acting honestly by the Church to which you profess to belong, and whose loaves you eat.

"Now," says Hooker, "where the Word of GOD leaveth the Church to make choice of her own ordinances, if against those things which have been received with great reason, or against such ordinances as the power and authority of that Church under which we live hath itself devised for the public good, or against the discretion of the Church in mitigating sometimes, with favourable equity, that rigour which otherwise the literal generality of ecclesiastical laws hath judged to be more convenient and meet; if, against all this, it should be free for men to reprove, to disgrace, to reject, at their own liberty, what they see done and practised according to order set down; if, in so great variety of ways as the wit of man is easily able to find out towards any purpose, and in so great liking as all men especially have unto those inventions whereby some one shall seem to have been more enlightened from above than many thousands, the Church did give every man license to follow what himself imagineth that 'GOD'S Spirit doth reveal' unto him, or what he supposeth that GOD is likely to have revealed to some special person whose virtues deserve to be highly esteemed ;—what other effect could hereupon ensue but the utter confusion of His Church under pretence of being taught, led, and guided by His Spirit? The gifts and graces whereof do so naturally all tend to common peace, that where such singularity is, they whose heart it possesseth ought to suspect it the more, inasmuch as if it did come of GOD, and should for that cause prevail with others, either with miraculous operation or with strong and invincible remonstrance and sound reason, such as whereby it might appear that GOD would indeed have all men's judgments give place unto it; whereas now the error and unsufficiency of their arguments do make it on the contrary side against them a strong presumption that GOD hath not moved their hearts to think such things as He hath not enabled them to prove" (bk. v. 10).

I could not but give you the whole measure of this transcendant good sense; what have you to say to it?

Ritualist. To say, why, that we can prove that our vestments are ancient, and that they were worn in these same Churches.

Catholic. Granted. But that is not the question. It is, that the present vestments, rites, and ceremonies commonly used in the English Church having come to be ancient by the sanction of three centuries, you must, according to Hooker and to common-sense, have very urgent reasons in order to change them wholly or in part. Better, godlier, and wiser men than either you or I, found not only edification in the rites and ceremonies of the Church as at present observed, but therein also trod their pathway to heaven, using them as channels of spiritual graces; why, then, are they not good enough for you also, and what is the urgent reason that leads you to adopt these innovations contrary to received custom?

Ritualist. But you know our vestments are symbolical; your surplice is not.

Catholic. Excuse me, the only real symbolism, as you shall see presently, is in the surplice. However, let your vestments be symbolical; what symbolism?

Ritualist. I do not exactly remember; but I know that one vestment of a certain colour means certain things, and that another form of dress of another colour means another thing, but I confess——

Catholic.——that I have forgotten my symbolism. What sort of benefit or edification, then, think ye, the congregation can possibly derive from fancies and inventions which are difficult even for you to remember? Since, however, that "signs must resemble the things they signify" is, we saw, the first requisite for an alteration in such signs, I must leave you to show that all your ceremonies, attitudes, postures, and genuflexions really represent something which they mean, and are therefore necessary; for, as I neither know nor understand them all, they are, to my mind, not only most distracting from real worship, but little else than a dumb show, and unmeaning to the congregation. Meanwhile, I will help you a little about your symbolism. As, however, I do not take the same comfort you do in things which—forgive me for saying so—seem, to say the least, frivolous and unmanly, in connection with the majesty and with the dignity of GOD'S worship, I have not studied them, and can only repeat, at second hand, what your own authorities say on the subject; and yet, not all of them, as I have not access to Goar, Habert, Bona, and other such works.

But first about colours.

"De vestium sacrarum colore tribus primis Ecclesiæ seculis usitato ob veterum monumentorum inopiam multa dicere, nobis haud integrum est; Recentiorum autem testimoniis nemo nisi rerum inter Christianos gestarum ignarus habebit fidem," says the learned Augustine; so that not only is it impossible to speak positively of colour during the first three centuries of the Church, but no one that is not ignorant of Church matters will add faith to what moderns say about it. "Sæculo IV. Vestes *candidas* in Liturgia adhibebant veteres, quod argumento nobis est eamdem in *antiquioribus* temporibus obtinuisse consuetudinem, præsertim cum color *albus* omnibus in sacris fuerit usitatus, quod copiose æque ac erudite P. Honoratus 1 c., tom. 2, l. 4, diss. 6, act 3, nobis commonstravit." But, since we have positive proof that priests wore white garments in the fourth century, we infer from it that those white vestments were in use before that time. Thus S. Gregory of Nazianzus, in his vision of the temple of Anastasia (tom. ii. oper. p. 78) represents deacons as clad in garments white as snow while standing around the altar: " *Niveis in vestibus*, ait, *adstabat turba ministra splendorem referens agminis angelici* (Aug. Krazer. de Colore Vest. Lit. p. 278, *et seq*. The italics are his here and in all extracts from his work). Likewise does S. Jerome speak of his own time (Adv. Pelag. Lib. i.) when he says, " *Quæ sunt inimicitiæ contra Deum si Tunicam habuero mundiorem, si Episcopus, Presbyter et reliquus ordo ecclesiasticus in administratione Sacramentorum candida in veste processerit*. Chrysostomus in Matth. Homil. 87, c. 6, ita sacros mystas admonet : *Idcirco vos Deus tanto voluit honore decorare, ut hæc diligentissime discernatis. Hæc est dignitas vestra, hæc stabilitas, hæc corona, non ut Tunicam induti candidissimam per Ecclesiam ambuletis*. Voluit quippe Ecclesia, ut altaris ministri et in *vestibus* imitarentur Angelos et sanctos in cœlis, qui amicti *stolis albis* ante Dominum assistant" (De Colore Vest. Liturgic. p. 278, *et seq*.). The intention of the Church having at all times been that her priests should, like angels, be clad in white robes while standing before the Lord. Also quoted by Hooker, bk. v. 29, 3.

To this our author adds "that even adversaries

do not dispute this;" while Dallæus (De Cultu Latin. Relig. l. viii. c. 14), who thinks the variety of colours in use now-a-days in the Romish Church agreeable to the eye, declares, nevertheless, that it was first introduced in the tenth century, being unknown in the primitive Church, and is only a Latin innovation. This our author attempts to disprove by the fact that in the windows of S. John Lateran, at Rome, erected in the seventh century, there are priests represented in coloured garments. Of this, however, others must judge; I have neither leisure nor mind for so unprofitable a pursuit. I may just add, however, that, towards the end of the twelfth century, there were four colours in use in the Romish Church: *white*, as emblem of innocence, for virgins; *red*, for apostles and martyrs; *green*, for Sundays and holidays; and *black*, for fast-days, Advent and Lent. Then *violet* was used twice in the year; until, in the fourteenth century, *black* was adopted exclusively for the service of the dead, and *violet* for days of fasting and penitence (*ibid.* De Col. Vestib. Lit. p. 278, *et seq.*). "Let us, however," adds to the purpose S. Clement Al., "ἐσθῆτι χρῆσθαι τῇ λιτῇ, χρόᾳ δὲ τῇ λευκῇ, wear a garment simple and white; and, renouncing what is artificial, deceitful, and untrue, let us embrace τὸ μονότροπον καὶ μονοπρόσωπον τῆς ἀληθείας, the artless manner and honest bearing of truth; for, as we show by our dress what we are, so also εἰρηνικοῖς ἄρα ἀνθρώποις καὶ φωτεινοῖς κατάλληλον τὸ λευκόν, does white, in sooth, become men who love peace and are without guile" (Pædag. lib. iii. p. 244). Thus far, then, you see that I have both taste, antiquity, authority, propriety, and Catholicity in favour of my white garment called surplice. But more of this anon.

Ritualist. And now about the vestments.

Catholic. As I said, I do not know much about them; I must, therefore, only repeat what your own friends say. You cannot wish for better authorities, or for fairer dealing. "Primum vestimentum nobis est *amictus*. Vestis *veteribus* incognita, sæculo demum vii. et viii., sensim in Ecclesiam inducta—ut *Birretum* sæculo xiii.—cujus *mysticæ* et *symbolicæ* significationes hæc sunt—ut presbyteri ponant *ore suo* custodiam; et caput amiciant *sacco pænitentiæ;* vel potiùs *spirituali galea* cooperiant." "The cope, then, was unknown to the ancient Church," says our authority, and was gradually introduced about the seventh, eighth, or perhaps thirteenth century; but the mystical and symbolical import thereof is (1) that the presbyters put a watch on their lips; or (2) that they cover themselves with sackcloth; or (3) that they wear a spiritual helmet.

The next sacerdotal vestment is "Tunica linea, quam a colore *albam* Latini vocarunt. Illam peculiare nobilium Romanorum fuisse ornamentum Vopiscus tradit; Ecclesia vero quæ vestem hanc candidam ministris sacris quam maxime convenire, judicabat, jam ab antiquissimis temporibus illam ex usu communi et profano ad *sacrum* traduxit, voluitque altaris ministros alba hac veste non tantum in *foro*, sed et in Ecclesia inter missarum solemnia esse indutos" (*ibid.*, p. 256). This white tunic, then, albe, or surplice, according to the Greek Church ('Ιερὰ κατήχ. p. 24), is meant to represent (1) the brightness of Christ's divine nature; (2) the innocence that becomes His priests; (3) the white garment in which Herod sent Him to Pilate; and (4) the brightness of angels as ministering servants of God around the altar; quoting the original of S. Gregory's N. words :—

οἱ δ' ἀρ' ὑποδρηστῆρες ἐν ἥμασι παμφανόωσιν
ἔστασαν, ἀγγελικῆς ἐικόνες ἀγλαΐης.

As regards the chasuble, "quemadmodum *alba*, ita et *casula sacerdotalis* antiquitus profana erat vestis," it was originally, like the albe, a secular garment worn by the laity. "Sæculo viii. Ecclesiorum prælatis nulla vestis gravitati et decentiæ Clericorum magis conveniens videbatur, quam casula, hinc illam Presbyteris et Diaconis pro veste *ordinaria et communi* omnino præscripserunt." But it came into general use only in the eighth century (*ib.* p. 257). It is the same as the Greek *Planeta*, and of various forms (*ib.* p. 308, *et seq.*)

"Sequitur *cingulum*, quod mystica significatione non caret; deinde *manipulus* qui sequiori demum ævo inter vestes *sacras* suum obtinuit locum. Alcuinus, Amalarius, aliique nobis unice testantur, habuisse quondam ministros Ecclesiæ sinistro brachio *linteum* quoddam obligatum, quo vultus sudorem et narium sordes abstergerent; et aliquando *sudarii* nomen tulit, nec non *sindonis, mappulæ,* etc. Nihil aliud est *nisi manus ornamentum*" (*ib.* p. 291, *et seq.*)

This maniple, then, originally used as a pocket-handkerchief, afterwards became a mere ornament of the hand, of various colours, and adorned with jingles of gold and precious stones, that stand in strange contrast as a symbol, "*doloris et fletus* qui in hac vita sustinendus, et manipulo quasi detergendus est" (*ib.* p. 297), of the sorrow and weeping which we have to endure in this life, and which are to be, as it were, wiped off with the maniple.

Ritualist. Really I did not know that.

Catholic. I don't suppose you did. There would yet be a great deal more to tell you about it; but time would fail. I only wonder any sensible man can be in earnest about such trifles and frivolities, especially in connection with the service of GOD and of His Church. May I ask you one question —are you in earnest?

Ritualist. What do you mean?

Catholic. Because I cannot think you are. Yet, only to show you how little this symbolism is " Catholic," and how far all those who put on this apparel are from agreeing as to the meaning thereof, hear what is the Greek symbolism of the maniples (ἐπιμάνικα and ὑπομάνικα),—" de quarum forma inter Orientales Christianos nihil certi affirmare possumus," says Renaudot (Lit. Or. vol. ii. p. 55). Not a word is said by the Greek Church about "sorrow and weeping;" for these maniples "are (1) the symbol of vigilance, (2) of diligence in performing the service of the altar, (3) of the binding of our Saviour's hands, (4) of the almighty power of GOD, who, with His hands, made all things" ('Ιερὰ κατήχ. *ib.*).

After such symbolism, I need go no further. I will, however, say a few words on the stole, in order to gratify you. "Vestes sacras ac liturgicas antiquitus *ejusdem* fuisse *formæ*, ac vestes laicorum communes et usitatas, ex decreto Stephani I. Rom. Pont. perspicue colligimus, qui anno 260 martyr occubuit." (De Vestis. Liturg. in genere p. 250, *et seq.*) Ast *stola* veteribus fuit *vestis manicata, et talaris ad terram usque defluens*, Judæis, Græcis et Romanis, imo omnibus gentibus usitatissima. Sed de hac veste nobis in præsenti sermo non est; sed de *orario*, quod sæculo demum viii. et ix. *stolæ* nomen accepit. Erat autem antiquitus *orarium*, linteolum, vel fascia *linea* urbanitatis causa a civibus Romanis ad vultus *sudorem* detergendum circa *collum* vel *humeros* gestari solita—antiquitus humeros tegebat—et brevi *singulare* Episcoporum, Presbyterorum et Diaconorum evasit *ornamentum*, dignitatis et jurisdictionis *symbolum*, cæpitque primo *coloribus* et *auro* ornari, dein non ampliùs ex lino sed ex serico, aliaque pretiosa confici materia." The stole, then, is, like the other vestments, a relic of the Roman laity, and was originally worn with sleeves. But about the eighth and ninth century the name of "stole" was given to the *orarium*, or the present "stole," which was originally a neck-handkerchief or scarf to wipe off the perspiration, that was worn sometimes on the right and sometimes on the left shoulder; and by the 38th Canon of the Synod of Toledo, it was to be plain, of no bright colour, and not ornamented with gold. This, too, had a mystical signification; it was the robe of immortality(*ib.* DeVestib. Liturg. inspec. p.299—307).

Here, again, the same vestment seems to convey a very different meaning in one part of the Catholic Church from what it does in another; for, if the stole be the ὠμοφόριον, then does it symbolise the "lost sheep" which the Good Shepherd brought back on His shoulders; and also the Cross which our Saviour carried, in order to remind those who wear this ὠμοφόριον (or stole) of the Cross they are to bear after Christ. So that West it is "a symbol of authority and of jurisdiction," and East one of 'lowliness and of profound humility;" assuredly symbolism is here at fault. If, however, the *stola* answers to the ἐπιτραχήλιον (you must forgive me for not being more learned in the matter), then does it symbolise "(1) the yoke of Christ, (2) the cord with which our Saviour was led away to Caiaphas, (3) the grace of the Holy Ghost coming from above, and (4) the scourge with which Pilate commanded our Lord to be scourged" ('Ιερα κατ. *ibid.* p. 24, 26). In either case the sign is not like the thing signified; and you must see that it is idle to talk of symbolism in connection with these vestments, since it is so purely imaginary that the same article of dress is made to be a symbol of opposite qualities, virtues, or duties, in different quarters of the Church. You may easily convince yourself of this by looking into the matter, when you will see, for instance, wherein the Armenian vestments differ from the Greek, the Greek from the Syrian, these from the Coptic, and these again from the Abyssinian, and all of them, more or less, from the Roman. And you will then appreciate the truth of what Renaudot says: "De vestimentorum illorum variis appellationibus et forma; accuratiùs et prolixiùs inquirere nullius utilitatis est, cùm nomina ipsa varias interpretationes tulerint ab Ægptiis, Syris et aliis—formam verò, quæ tot sæculorum decursu mutationem haud dubiè passa est, delineare ex conjecturis nihil juvat." Then as to what the Greeks have written on the subject, and as to their mysticism thereon, it bears in no wise on Oriental vestments; for neither is the form nor the colour of vestments the same among them. Sometimes the stole is one way, sometimes another; the chasuble also is of one or of many colours, with or without the streamers common in the Greek Church. "Sed in istis diutiùs immorari non videtur operæ pretium, cùm antiqua forma ex autorum descriptionibus non satis intelligi possit" (Renaud. Lit. Or. vol. ii., p. 55, and vol. i., p. 180, *et seq.*, and Dulaur. Egl. Arm. p. 182). No wonder, in sooth, if the honest and sober-minded Hooker should speak of such things, however much esteemed by certain men, as "of things that have lately sprung up for complements, rites, and ceremonies of Church actions, and are, in truth, for the greatest part, such silly things that very easiness doth make them hard to be disputed of in a serious manner" (Ecc. Pol. b. v. ded. 3).

As it must be evident to yourself that this symbolism of your vestments is a myth, purely imaginary, without a shadow of truth, and a fond invention to beguile certain weak and listless minds, you will, I trust, allow me to consider sufficient what I have just quoted about colours and symbolism, both of which appear to me very trifling and very unworthy of serious consideration. If either subject, or both, had been settled by the common consent of the whole Church Catholic, it would, to say the least, command the greatest respect; but what is a sensible and sober-minded man to do when so much stress is laid on such apparent frivolities, on which no two sections of the so-called Catholic Church agree? I must therefore decline further treating the subject in connection with the solemn service of the Eucharist, as jarring with my feelings of reverence for that Holy Sacrament.

Yet I will, for your own gratification, give you one

more bit of your favourite symbolism with reference, not to liturgical, but to episcopal vestments. Thomas Aquinas, or his commentator, Gorcomius writing on the subject, says (Supplem. Pt. III. Q. 40, art. 7)—" Episcopus habet super Sacerdotem nova vestimenta, quæ sunt Caligæ, Sandalia, Succinctorium, Tunica, Dalmatica, Mitra, Chirotecæ, Annulus, et Baculus. By the hose (Caligæ) is meant an upright walk in life; by the sandals (Sandalia), or shoes, that cover the foot, is meant contempt for earthly things; by the girdle (Succinctorium), with which the stole is fastened with the albe, is meant the love of what is honest; by the tunic (Tunica) is meant perseverance, inasmuch as we read that Joseph wore a tunic that reached down to his heels, that represent the end of life; by the dalmatic (Dalmatica) is meant liberality in works of charity; by the gloves (Chirotecæ), cautiousness in action; by the mitre (Mitra), the knowledge of both the Old and New Testaments, whence it has two horns (duo cornua); then the staff (Baculus) betokens the shepherd's care, and how he ought to recall the wandering, represented by the crook at the top of the staff; how to support the weak, told by the staff itself; and how to goad on the slothful, wherefore the staff is armed with a spike at the end; while his ring symbolises the sacraments of Faith, wherewith the Church is betrothed to Christ, for bishops hold in the Church the place of Christ." You must agree with me that probably few bishops know all they are supposed to carry when arrayed in their robes.

Ritualist. Possibly.

Catholic. The less so as several of these articles of dress are comparatively modern: the mitre, for instance, was unknown before the tenth or twelfth century (De Veste Episcop., pp. 321—333). But, as I cannot give you credit for being in earnest in this case, I begin to suspect there must be some other reason to make you hold on to your "Ritualism," which you see, and might yet see much plainer, is neither "Catholic" nor "Apostolic;" for I cannot believe that you or any other sensible English man could, in this nineteenth century of light and knowledge, be in earnest about such childish matters, offspring of the darkness and superstition of the Middle Ages. If, as S. Paul tells us, "the kingdom of GOD is not meat and drink," much less is it copes and maniples, "but righteousness and peace and joy in the Holy Ghost;" none of which good fruits your "revival of vestments" has yet wrought. Seeing, then, that we cannot speak seriously of this symbolism of vestments and of colours, still less of their Catholicity, what else is there to make you thank GOD you are a "Ritualist" and not as other men are?

Ritualist. I told you before that, without, as you say, thanking GOD I am a Ritualist, I find that outward show more conducive to devotion than your cold, monotonous, Anglican services.

Catholic. I am sorry to find they produce such different impression upon you from what they do upon me; and still more so, that your devotion requires the help of meretricious ornaments and of needless, if not altogether unmeaning, ceremonies. But we have talked enough. We will further discuss the matter at our next meeting.

III.—OF THE ENGLISH CHURCH, OF THE RE-UNION OF CHRISTENDOM, AND OF THE HOLY EUCHARIST.

*ATHOLIC.* You were saying that your vestments and ceremonies were more to your mind as being more showy and more demonstrative than the Anglican surplice and simple worship.

Ritualist. Yes; I think that more pomp than you like is best.

Catholic. I agree with you on principle that we cannot show too much respect and veneration for the service of GOD's Church, within due limits of propriety, of good taste, and of good sense. In building the house where "His honour dwelleth," we ought to do it as an act of worship; and, had we the means, we might lay the floor of agate, rear the pillars of jasper, carve the capitals of silver, build the walls of alabaster, make the roof of cedar and sandal wood, and frame the windows with rubies and amethysts, with crystals, sapphires, and emeralds set in a network of gold. Yet He who inhabits eternity, and whom no house made with hands can contain, needs none of these things which Himself has made, even though He condescend to accept them as offerings at our hands; since He promises "to be in the midst of two or three that are met in His name." So also as regards His worship. As no human pomp, no costly array, no magnificence ever could reach up to the footstool of His Majesty on high, did He, on the one hand, with regard to the pompous ritual of His sanctuary, command that, when the high priest appeared before Him in the holiest, he should strip himself of his robes of scarlet and purple, and enter clad in his white tunic alone; and, on the other hand, under the new covenant, did He declare that "He seeketh for His worshippers such as worship in spirit and in truth," so that, when they come together, "things be done decently and in order;" for He is "not a GOD of confusion, but of peace, as in all the churches of the saints."

Since, then, His public service cannot be performed "decently and in order" without a definite ritual strictly and uniformly observed by one and the same company of men, how is it that there is no "Catholic" ritual—no one set outline of outward form of worship for the whole Church Catholic, defined and instituted by the Apostles at the same time that they taught the Church that there is only "one body and one

Spirit, even as all her members are called in one hope of their calling; one Lord, one faith, one baptism; one God and Father of all, who is above all, and through all, and in them all" (Eph. iv. 4—6)? Simply because, "as God is no respecter of persons, but in every nation he that feareth Him, and worketh righteousness, is accepted of Him" (Acts x. 34, 35), so also did He leave the externals of religion, the outward forms of His worship, to these same men of all nations to settle, according to their national habits, tastes, and ideas, so long as these forms are in order, and so long as the ceremonies have a meaning tending to edification. For He gives us plainly to understand that neither vain repetitions nor a service performed in a language not understood of the people are agreeable to Him, simply because neither the one nor the other has any meaning at all. Therefore, were it possible, it would be as much against wisdom and common sense to thrust upon the English people a foreign ritual and worship alien in form and in spirit to the actual taste, ideas, and habits of the nation, as it is absurd to make Bengalee converts sit on benches and walk in shoes and stockings, as if they could not listen far better while sitting at ease on their own mats, according to custom, and come, as they are wont, barefoot to their thatched bungalows.

Ritualist. But you seem to forget that these forms and ceremonies now called "Ritualism" are, in fact, Anglican, and according to a law that never was repealed.

Catholic. Are they Anglican ? and whence came they to Anglia? Under what circumstances, and under what rule, did they continue in use? and how is it that for three hundred years they have been forgotten? Is it not because, being thoroughly at variance with the plain good taste and innate sober sense of the English character, that detests the trappings and the frivolous show certain foreign nations delight in, the moment the thraldom ceased under which these foreign Romish vestments and ceremonies were introduced and kept up, and the people had an opportunity of following the dictates of its own national taste, than these vestments and ceremonies were abandoned and at once, or nearly so, doomed to oblivion; and the real Anglican, or English service, that stands alone for simplicity and decorum, for worship and reverence, when duly performed, was made to take their place? The very fact, then, that those foreign vestments and ceremonies are obsolete, and have ceased altogether for the last three hundred years, must condemn them at once as un-English in the opinion of every sensible man. Moreover, the fact that the law that sanctioned them never was repealed does not, assuredly, prove that it is still in force, but rather that it was needless to repeal a law which the common consent of the whole nation and the daily usage of three centuries have, to all intents and purposes, made a dead letter. Therefore are those vestments and ceremonies not lawful, even though in law they may be legal; and, since they are assuredly not expedient at the present time, the revival of them shows neither wisdom nor judgment on the part of those who work at it.

Speaking of his own days, Hooker says to the purpose, "In regard to the great hurt which the Church did receive by a number of things established, the Reformers saw it best to cut off presently such things as might in that sort be extinguished without danger, leaving the rest to be abolished by disusage through tract of time. For there is not any positive law of men, whether it be general or particular, received by formal express consent, as in councils, or by secret approbation, as in customs it cometh to pass, but the same may be taken away if occasion serve. Even as we all know, that many things generally kept heretofore are now, in like sort, generally unkept and abolished everywhere" (bk. iv. 14, 3—5). In proof of this, what say ye to putting now in force certain obsolete Acts, as, *e.g.*, the Act for preventing Popery and other sects, passed in consequence of the doings of friar Faithful Cummins, who was rewarded by Pope Pius V. for having pretended to inveigh against him and preached dissent out of spite against the Church, in Queen Elizabeth's reign, "an Act which enjoined all people, from ten years old and upwards, not having lawful impediment, to repair every Sunday to hear Divine service, under penalty of forfeiting twelve pence for every default"—that never was repealed, and still is as much law as that on which you rest the legality of your innovations?

Ritualist. Yet, apart from all that, you must grant me that one feels the want of something more than is found in the Church of England as it now is.

Catholic. I readily grant you much; I grant you that one's heart often sickens at the way in which the Church is treated by the State, that seems to take pleasure in insulting or in slighting her, and in raising the arm of flesh, intended of GOD as a protection to her, only to molest her, and not to defend "the Faith once delivered to the saints" which is her faith. I grant you that it is impossible to love the Church without feeling at times aggrieved at the apparently arbitrary, if not oppressive, measures whereby the civil power attempts to force upon her Arianism, Socinianism, scepticism, and infidelity, though, of course, in vain; for gold is not soiled by mud cast upon it. I also grant you that the increasing immorality and want of principle in the nation at large, the utter recklessness of thought—or, I should rather say, of talk—and "the love of many waxing cold, because of the iniquity that abounds," seem to point to the time "when the Son of man cometh, shall He find faith in the earth?" And it all leaves an aching void within, a feeling of isolation and of awe at the coming judgments, that may lead one instinctively to look for companionship and for greater union with the Church Catholic as a body.

But your copes and your maniples will not do it. We want a better stay than that at a time when "men's hearts fail them for fear" and many seem "carried about with every wind of doctrine, by the sleight of men and cunning craftiness whereby they lie in wait to deceive," as in the days of the Apostles, and when "the foundations of the earth seem out of course," as in the time of David; for the Church always was and always will be militant here on earth. And this our stay is: "My grace is sufficient for thee; for my strength is made perfect in weakness." This keeps our faith from failing, and our love from dying; this nerves our arms for the fight and our hearts for the conflict that we must endure—if we be faithful. Whither, then, should we go for greater union? To Rome? to Greece? that hate each other with implacable hatred, and both of which hold articles of faith and doctrines which no "Catholic" Christian can receive. If we join either—seeing we cannot join both—we shall either not be on speaking terms with the other, or at war with all the rest, and thus, in fact, far less at peace and less united than we are even at present, by belonging to neither. Better by far seek union among our own selves, and be found doing our duty when our Master comes.

So that for you to leave the Anglican branch of the Church Catholic, which is not only as Catholic and as pure, but even purer than any other, only because it has to struggle with the world—for the vision of unity, and peace, and union in a Catholic or universal abode of heavenly freedom and purity here on earth, shows so little knowledge of things as they really are, and such simplicity, that I must either pity or excuse it in you, young as you are and inexperienced. As I know more of it than you do, let me guard you against what looks to me like going or floundering after a will-o'-the-wisp, or, if you like it better, like hankering after a day-dream that must end in disappointment. For where on earth is there a Church free from human infirmities, passions, and corruption? and where shall we find peace here below if we be soldiers of Him who "came not to send peace, but a sword"? If Church history tells true, not only has the Church always had to struggle with the world around, but she has also been at war with herself. So that no change will benefit you.

If, on the other hand, you object to a State Church, only reflect, and, like a sensible man, you will find that a Church should be national, and is made such on the soundest principle; so that whatever inconveniences result therefrom are defects inseparable from everything human, but not the real working of the system. For a national Church is, in fact, a public and national acknowledgment on the part of the Civil Power (1) that the State cannot subsist without fellowship with the Church as channel of GOD'S blessings, and (2) that it is the duty of the State to secure a knowledge of the Christian Faith to the people, as subjects of the realm. No other principle is either safe or sound, and none other can stand. It is the principle of the theocracy—not of a civil power ruled by ecclesiastical laws, that has brought the Roman State to decrepitude—but the wedding of the civil and of the ecclesiastical powers together for their mutual help and comfort. This union has made England great; to divorce it will assuredly make her small. For to say, as some do, that a "Liberal State" should have no national Church and support all sects alike, is, you must own, to say neither more nor less than that, as regards the State, it need have no Church, no good spirit to animate it, and, as regards GOD, that He may be worshipped anyhow or not at all. You must therefore excuse me for saying that I look upon every Englishman who leaves his Church, either for Rome or for Dissent, except it be for some more cogent reason than I can understand, as wanting in loyalty to his country.

Ritualist. Oh!——

Catholic. So it appears to me. When I see, on the one hand, how entirely the welfare of this State depends on GOD'S blessing, and how the real prosperity and greatness of the nation rest on the righteousness which has exalted it—for, without contradiction or boasting, England is the most religious country on earth—and not on the fleets of ironclads or of merchantmen that are sent to sea, I look upon every individual act of desertion that tends to weaken the bonds of Church and State as disloyal to the country. It may gratify one's pride, one's self-will, one's bumptiousness rashly to cut asunder these bonds in one's own individual case; but that, let me tell you, is neither wise nor charitable; neither for the glory of GOD, nor for the good of men. As long as the pure gold of the Catholic Faith in the Church is left unalloyed, as long as her Ritual is left intact in doctrine, and her Clergy are allowed freely to preach the Gospel, there can be no reason for leaving her. When, however, the gold of that Faith is put into the crucible and alloyed, and the English Clergy are made by law to teach error or heresy, then will it be time to part. But that is not yet. As long as the English Church has her pure and simple Ritual—the purest and best of any—I speak knowingly—the soul of which is to promote the worship of GOD "in spirit and in truth," and her Clergy are not obliged to teach and to preach false doctrine against their conscience,—it seems hasty, wrong, and disloyal in any of the English Clergy to leave their Church. If so be darkness around them increase, let their light shine all the brighter; if it be true light, some few, or even many, will surely come and rejoice at it, in a land like this, where the instincts of the people, when let alone, are always towards their Church.

Ritualist. You take a very different view of it from what I do.

Catholic. Very likely. For this reason, among others, can I feel no respect for the young brood of unfledged papists among the Clergy called Ritualists, who, in defiance of the very authority to which they pledged themselves to obey, care not what disturbance, what schism they create; but, on the contrary, rather glory in it so long as they can gratify their own private and individual fancies and oddities, and get others to follow them. No movement can be for good that begins so badly. It may, as it rolls along, gather numbers; for when has it been otherwise with revivals of gewgaws and pageants, that are sure to attract those who care for such things? This, however, is not the life of religion. You must prove to me why the fumes of incense, coloured copes, and embroidered maniples, with bowings and mutterings, set aside for 300 years as useless, can all at once become indispensable to the worship of GOD, and to true and living religion, ere I give up my own opinion of your "Ritualism," which appears to me to be nothing less than an audacious piece of arrogance on the part of some of the Clergy, who, withal, strike one as not particularly nice in their ideas of honesty, while they pretend to be Anglicans in name, but in reality teach Romish doctrines and, maybe, secretly give their allegiance to the Church of Rome. Have you, then, received a dispensation for pretending to be what you are not?

Ritualist. I will not get angry, though I think you smite rather hard. But you know, as well as I do, that the Bishops, as a body, do little for the Church. One, it is true, set to the whole bench the example of earnestness and of single-mindedness in the discharge of his duty, when he tried, at all risks, and with fearful odds against him, to drive heresy from his diocese. He failed, as, indeed, it was likely he would; but he got what was even better than partial success in this case—the answer of a good conscience that he had done his duty to his Master and to his people. But he stands alone. A few others may be active, harmless men, fair scholars, and good preachers; but, as a body, where is their unanimity, their boldness, their earnestness, and disinterestedness in the defence of the Church—where? The spasmodic doings of your Church look to me more like the jerks of a child's toy than like the even working of the members of the same body. Under such circumstances, may we not take upon ourselves to do one thing as well as another without consulting our Bishops?

Catholic. If I hit hard at your "Catholic symbolism," you certainly give it back in kind. I own all you say about the general state of things in the Church. I feel, as you do, the jerks to which you allude, and I should, indeed, wish it otherwise.

But, as the perfect union and unity of which you are dreaming are only for the Church when Christ's body perfected in heaven, I am prepared for those "jerks" and for that "spasmodic action" which are inevitable in a State Church, and in any Church on earth. And I would rather bear them than sever the Church from the State; because, not only would the State suffer from it, but also because the Church, when left to herself, would be subject to worse passions, and to yet more fitful jerks. At least so does the history of the Church tell me. While "of the Church Militant here in earth," I must be ready to endure contradiction, and to bear the heat and toil of the day, and, like a good soldier, to fight, not as beating the air, but so that I may please Him who has called me to be a soldier. I do not, therefore, see how any of these human infirmities which are inseparable from the earthly state of the Church this side heaven can justify you in breaking the fifth commandment, which, to my mind, is as binding in all ecclesiastical matters between you and him whom you deliberately chose for your spiritual Father, as between you and your natural father; let alone common courtesy. I really cannot understand how you, who talk so much about "Catholic Church and unity," can pretend to begin your new life of "Catholic obedience" by disobeying your spiritual Father, whose claim to Catholicity is prior to your own. What, think ye, would S. Ignatius have thought of you?

III.—Of the English Church, &c.

Ritualist. But you always assume that I have left the Anglican Church. I have done nothing of the sort; I still belong to it.

Catholic. Do you? Then am I to understand that you asked your Bishop's consent for all your innovations, and that he granted it?

Ritualist. At all events he has not said anything.

Catholic. And you construe that into approval on his part, and obedience on yours? How, then, do you understand these words, said generally by the Catholic and Apostolic Church, τὸν οὖν ἐπίσκοπον δῆλον ὅτι ὡς αὐτὸν τὸν Κύριον δεῖ προσβλέπειν, "It is, then, evident that you are to look upon the Bishop as upon the Lord" (S. Ignat. ad Eph. vi., and ad Trall. ii.); more definitely to the laity: ὑμεῖς ἄνευ τοῦ ἐπισκόπου, καὶ τῶν πρεσβυτέρων μηδὲν πράσσετε· μηδὲ πειράσητε εὐλογόν τι φαίνεσθαι ἰδίᾳ ὑμῖν, "Do nothing without the Bishop and the Presbyters, neither do you of your own selves attempt to think anything reasonable independently of them" (*ibid.* 7); then more especially to deacons: "Sotio the deacon, and my fellow-servant, of whom I have joy, ὅτι ὑποτάσσεται τῷ ἐπισκόπῳ ὡς χάριτι Θεοῦ, καὶ τῷ πρεσβυτερίῳ ὡς νόμῳ Ἰησοῦ Χριστοῦ, because he submits himself to the Bishop as to the grace of GOD, and to the presbytery as to the law of Jesus Christ" (*ibid.* 2). As to the Presbyters, that Father looked upon them as "the presbytery," inseparable from the Bishop, without whom they would, of course, do nothing; he does not, therefore, give them individually the warning not to act independently; but the Thirty-ninth Canon of the Apostles, that, come whence it will, is of authority in the Catholic (Greek) Church, is explicit on this point: Οἱ πρεσβύτεροι, καὶ Διάκονοι, ἄνευ γνώμης τοῦ Ἐπισκόπου μηδὲν ἐπιτελείτωσαν. Αὐτὸς γάρ ἐστιν ὁ πεπιστευμένος τὸν λαὸν τοῦ Κυρίου, καὶ ὑπὲρ τῶν ψυχῶν αὐτῶν λόγον ἀπαιτηθησόμενος. "Let neither priests nor deacons do aught without the Bishop's advice. For he has in charge the people of the Lord, and of him will the Lord ask an account."

Ritualist. Very good; but that was in olden times; in these days of freedom——

Catholic.——of freedom—of license, you mean. But I thought it was with you *quod ubique, quod semper, quod ab omnibus?*

Ritualist. So it is, of course, but, don't you see, by means of certain constructions—we may adapt it to the times, and thus follow them.

Catholic. Follow them! why, you are doing your utmost to bring us back to some three hundred years ago.

Ritualist. It is of no use going on like this; you know my meaning perfectly well.

Catholic. I really do not. How is it possible to reconcile this *quod ubique, quod semper*, with a dispensation from episcopal jurisdiction, when this runs counter of your own wishes?

Ritualist. Well, how do you expect I can continue in the same fold with your Broad Church, and Narrow Church, Low Church, and No Church? It is a perfect Noah's Ark.

Catholic. And, pray, what else is the Church on earth but Noah's Ark? I will not quote Greek Fathers, whom you do not like so well as Latin ones; but have you forgotten S. Augustine's words, "Arca —procul dubio figura est peregrinantis in hoc sæculo Civitatis Dei, hoc est, Ecclesiæ, quæ fit salva per lignum;" "Et fieri quidem, potest, ut et nobis quispiam et alius alio exponat hæc aptius: dum tamen ea quæ dicuntur, ad hanc de qua loquimur, Dei civitatem, in hoc sæculo maligno tanquam in diluvio peregrinante ne omnia referantur. Hoc etiam de cæteris quæ hic exponenda sunt, dixerim, quia etsi non uno disserantur modo, ad unam tamen Catholicæ fidei concordiam revocanda sunt?" (De. Civ. Dei. lib. xv. c. xvi)., and those of S. Cyprian (Epist. lxix.) quoting S. Peter, "Quod et Petrus— probans, et contestans unam arcam Noe typum fuisse unius Ecclesiæ;" to which S. Ambrose (De Voc. Gent. lib. c. 4), "Illâ mirandæ capacitatis arcâ universi generis animalium quantum reparationis aderat, recepisse, congregatura ad se omne hominum genus Ecclesia figuratur." I grant you that in this Church things are not altogether as we might wish, but where and when has the Church of Christ been otherwise than mixed and militant? Her rest is not here; and not until her warfare is accomplished. At all events, we of the Anglican Church have a pure ritual; we have neither error, heresy, nor quack doctrines forced upon us as articles of faith, or at least as dogmas to teach our people, and we have the protection of the law, and the goodwill and affection of all the better and more sensible part of the nation—so many privileges, that ought to be for us incentives to the more faithful discharge of our duty as servants of Christ, and as ministers of His Church.

Ritualist. All very good; but don't you think THE CATHOLIC CHURCH is a grand idea—the reunion of Christendom, the——

Catholic. I agree with you that to look upon the whole Church of Christ as washed in His Blood, and purchased by Him at that inestimable price, is a grand, the grandest idea we can dwell upon. But what has that to do with copes, maniples, incense, and symbolism? Do you mean to tell me, first, that we of the Anglican Church are not of the Church Catholic; and, secondly, that if you joined the Church of Rome to-morrow—if you do not already belong to it, for I cannot make you out—you would be a whit nearer Catholic union and unity, the communion of saints and happiness, than you are at present, poor deluded man?

Do look before you leap. From what you let me guess, your idea of Catholicity seems to be a kind of spiritual *nirvána*, or final emancipation into an ideal world where neither human passions rule nor dissension prevails, into a region of saints in chasubles and virgins in white, and I know not what else. Ask, then, first some honest man who joined the Church of Rome and then left it, to tell you whether, on the whole, he was so very sure he had reached the land of delights; then ask a Greek, also of the Church Catholic, what he thinks of that of Rome; then, again, take a Greek of another section of the Greek Church, and ask him in what sort of love and of union he lives with his brethren of the opposite party. After that take a Gregorian Armenian and a united one, and see how they feel towards each other; then step over among the Jacobites, Nestorians, and Maronites of the Syrian Church, who are at daggers drawn one with another; and at last question the Coptic Church, all but anathematised on certain points by the rest; thence go down to Abyssinia and witness there the lowest estate of the Catholic Church; and at last look into the utter disorder and arbitrary rule of certain Reformed Churches. That will give you a more correct idea of the Church Catholic than you seem to have; and if your feelings agree with mine, you will then return from your Catholic excursion a wiser and better man, more than ever thankful for the light, for the knowledge, for the truth, for the peace and quiet, even such as they are—for the ritual, for the services, and for the really Catholic spirit of the Anglican Church than ever you were before your foreign trip.

And as to greater union and unity in the Church of Rome than in what you are pleased to call

Noah's Ark—"Verum, O DEUS bone"—"Good GOD!" says Bishop Jewell, "who, then, are those Papists who reproach us with our dissensions? Why, then, is their own Albertus Pighius at loggerheads with their Cajetan, Thomas with Lombardus; Scotus at war with Thomas, Ochamus opposed to Scotus, and Alliensis to Ochamus? and why are the Nominalists at daggers drawn with the Realists? Those men never agree among themselves, except, perhaps, like Herod and Pilate, or like the Pharisees and the Sadducees of old against Christ. Let them go home, then, and first make peace among themselves." Had things been half as bad in the Ark, Noah would never have come out of it alive. But Jewell, the brave Jewell, knew all about it; he carried the day at Westminster Abbey, and helped to free the Church of England from the same trammels into which your party wish to bring her back. Have you read his Apology? If not, do read it; and hearken to a lesson of homely but true wisdom taught me by one of my poor labourers.

One day, while going through my parish, I met a man leaning against a gate, with his hands in his pockets, and looking very much, as they say, "down in the mouth."

"What is the matter with you, Jem?" said I; "you look out of sorts."

"Why, sir, wages be so low, and times be so tir'ble 'ard."

"Why, then, don't you go abroad—to Australia?

There you will find more work and better wages."

"To Hástrela? So I d' hear. But I'll tell you what, sir: I d' know how it be here; but I don't know how it be there. So I'll bide here."

"You are right, my man. Here is a shilling for your good sense."

Ritualist. Do you mean to apply this to my going, as you think, over to Rome?

Catholic. Believe that man, and "bide where you be," and don't go to "Hástrela," not even though they offer you a free passage thither. You will not better yourself by going anywhere away from the Church of Whitgift, Laud, Barrow, Jewell, Taylor, Lightfoot, Hooker, Beveridge, and other such worthies. They were true Catholics, and are now brilliant stars in the firmament of Heaven.

Ritualist. I am not yet gone.

Catholic. Not gone, perhaps; but are you not in reality going in your Popish ways? Bear with me, however, yet a while, and hearken.

The Church here on earth is like the bow drawn on the cloud, which is made up of bands of various colours, distinct and defined, all of which are of the light, though not one of them be the light itself. As the light comes from heaven, so also does the Truth; and as the light refracted in the drops of rain produces these bands of colour, so also does the Truth when refracted in the minds of men of divers nations. Some of those bands are of a warmer and brighter colour than others, in proportion as the light in them is less refracted. Thus red is warmer and brighter than purple; still, they are, one and all, only refracted light, and not the light itself. So, also, is the pure Truth among men. It must of necessity be more or less refracted, since the human mind can neither grasp nor hold it either pure or whole; and, by being thus refracted, it has formed the several nationally distinct branches of the Church Catholic; among which the Reformed Anglican Church is the red ray, of purer, warmer, and of less refracted light than the rest. But the very diversity of these several bands of colour that agree together to form a beautiful image, is an emblem of peace; for green does not strive to become red, but, with red and purple, waits until they all again merge into the pure light of the sunbeam.

So also with the Church Catholic; that must continue in separate branches as long as she is on earth. As no two or three colours in the bow, nor any number short of the full seven, if mixed together, would make light, but only create a dingy mixture far worse than the original colours, so also no two, no three, or four, or more of these national sections or branches of the Church Catholic, joined together, would create aught but confusion, and would make of this partial reunion a mass worse assorted, and also darker than were the several branches or bands before they were mingled together. This local and partial reunion would not be a bit more Catholic, nor a bit more true—probably less so; and this, simply because we shall never have pure Catholic truth, like pure light, until all the bands of Christ's Church on earth become one with Him in heaven. There only—not here below—shall we be "one with Him, even as He and His Father are one;" for there and then only shall we see Him even as He is, and know Him as we are known of Him.

This, you see, bears upon "the re-union of Christendom," to which you alluded; a good and pious wish, indeed, as we are taught by our Saviour to say, "Thy kingdom come," but, at the same time, little else than a day-dream when taken in hand as it is by men who think they can achieve it. "It is not for them to know the times and seasons which the Father hath put in His own power." In His own good time His Church shall be one in Him—not until then. Meanwhile His servants will show greater wisdom in giving heed, every man for himself, to his own daily work, so as to be found at his post, with his loins girt about and his lamp burning, when his Master comes. Not all our efforts will hasten the day; and, when that day comes, not all our efforts could hinder it.

Ritualist. Perhaps not; but you see——

Catholic. Well, shall I tell you what I see? I see that you are much too sensible and too sober-minded a man, young though you be, to advocate this Ritualism, these vain ceremonies and gaudy vestments, either because they are "Catholic and Apostolic," since you know perfectly well that they are neither the one nor the other, or on account of their symbolical meaning, of which you also feel you, as a sensible man, cannot speak seriously. There must, then, be some other and more weighty reason for your saying that you felt "revived" by the display of vestments and by the fumes of incense at S. ———. Is it, perhaps, that your imagination gets the better of your judgment, and that, in your mind, you connect these pontifical vestments with "the daily sacrifice at the altar," and thus work yourself up to think—for you cannot believe it—that you eat and drink materially the Body and Blood of Christ, there slain and consecrated for you?

Ritualist. Do you not, then, believe in His Real Presence in that Holy Sacrament?

Catholic. I do; because I believe in "reality" apart from visible matter. I believe in the reality of a spirit as I do in the person and real existence of the Holy Ghost. I therefore believe in the Real Presence of Christ in the Holy Eucharist, as taught in the ritual of my Church, which is also according to the light of my own common sense. I believe "that the Body and Blood of Christ are verily and indeed taken and received by the faithful in the Lord's Supper;" understanding "verily and indeed" to mean "really and truly,"

III.—The Mystery of the Holy Eucharist.

but spiritually and not materially, through the efficacy of the Holy Spirit, whom, we pray, in this sacrament, as well as in that of Baptism, τὸν φιλάνθρωπον Θεὸν—ἐξαποστεῖλαι ἐπὶ τὰ προκείμενα, ἵνα ποιήσῃ τὸν μὲν ἄρτον, σῶμα Χριστοῦ, τὸν δὲ οἶνον αἷμα Χριστοῦ, "our benevolent GOD to send upon the elements, that He (the Holy Spirit) may make the bread the Body of Christ, and the wine His Blood," says S. Cyril of Jerusalem (Catech. Mystag. v.).

But this is entirely spiritual, and, as S. Chrysostom says, " seen διὰ τῶν ὀφθαλμῶν τῆς πίστεως, with the eyes of faith" (De Sacerd. lib. iii. 4); that is, "by the faithful." And this, again, not by faith in the dictates of this or of that teacher, but by one's own faith in the Spiritual Presence of Christ, and thus, also, in the efficacy of that Holy Sacrament, according to the estimate of that Presence, and to the proportion of faith in it—whether it be much or little—of every individual "faithful" partaker of the Lord's Supper. For it is evident that in this HOLY MYSTERY, which Joh. Maro says "has been hidden from everlasting, and is out of the reach of all human understanding" (Joh. M. in Lamy Diss. p. 176) one man cannot see deeper than another; for a Mystery is a Mystery to all men alike. So that, after all, the benefit every "faithful" receives from it, is only according to his own faith, and not according to that of his priest; whatever this one may say, and by what means soever he may attempt to determine the Real Presence of Christ in the Eucharist.

So truly is it a Mystery, to be taken and enjoyed only by faith and not by the intellect, that (1) our communion one with another in that Sacrament is not direct or immediate, but mediate through our individual intercourse with Him who is the Head of us members; that (2) there is hardly one of the earlier Fathers, whether Greek, Armenian, or Syrian, from whose writings one may not either twist or deduce, on the one hand, the bare memorial of Calvin's school, or, on the other hand, the material doctrine of the Church of Rome—so much did they feel on that Mystery, and so little did they understand it. Wherefore (3) even the Apostles did not venture beyond calling themselves "ministers of Christ, and stewards of the mysteries of God" (1 Cor. iv. 1, 2), adding "that it is required in stewards that a man be found faithful" in his management and dispensing of property not his own. Now such Mysteries as the Sacraments are not the priest's own; he holds them in trust, only to administer, and not to make them; but they are deep, unsearchable Mysteries; the property of Him who alone ordered, knows, and understands their whole bearing, meaning, and working.

To all of us, men, they are Mysteries;—and thus, for any one to presume to define, and to draw a line of what is or of what is not in them, is neither more nor less than arrogance and presumption, if it be not downright imposture. For no man can pretend to dogmatise on a subject which is unsearchable, and therefore as much hidden from him as from his fellows, without assuming a knowledge, and thereby also an authority, which he does not and cannot have. This is, however, what the Church of Rome has done, cutting the matter short by her doctrine of Transubstantiation; and thereby assuming a knowledge, and thus an authority, over the simple and the ignorant which she neither has nor can have, rather than make the confession, too galling for her arrogance, that neither she, nor any other Church, ever solved this Mystery, and that the Church in heaven can alone solve it. Yet that is what you, Ritualists, are trying to do; your conscience, all the while, rebuking you for asserting that about which you feel you know nothing. For, say what you will, so truly are we to walk by faith here on earth, that we have no other stay, even in the Bread and Wine that are the visible or outward part of the Sacrament, through which, mysteriously and mystically, our Saviour condescends to be more especially present and to commune with us, not visibly, but spiritually; as He is also, though in a more general way, present "where two or three are met together in His name;" and with His Church "always even unto the end of the world."

Therefore to invest this Holy Mystery with a material form, and to teach against Scripture, reason, and analogy that the bread we eat and the wine we drink are materially the Body and Blood of Christ, is, to my mind, so gross and so derogatory from the unsearchable influences of the Holy Spirit in that Sacrament, and from the Majesty thereof, as to border on the sensual and profane. As I cannot follow throughout the process by which even the food I take is turned into blood, and thus maintains life in my body, much less can I pretend to trace the means by which GOD'S Holy Spirit works through the spiritual food of the Body and Blood of my Saviour. But, as I feel that nourishment keeps my body in life, by my own consciousness of that life, so also does the Holy Spirit bear witness with my own spirit, through that Sacrament, of the life it imparts to my soul and spirit. I therefore believe in the Real Presence of Christ in that Holy Sacrament, while I shrink with horror at the very thought of its being done in a material form.

Ritualist. But our Saviour said, "Take, eat; this is my body given for you." These words seem plain enough in their natural sense.

Catholic. As I said, I hardly like to discuss so profound a mystery, lest I should inadvertently tread on holy and forbidden ground. I must, however, say—I trust, as I mean it, most reverently—that I do not understand how you can plead for a literal interpretation of those words. A moment ago you seemed to wonder that I did not stretch my imagination so far as to see in a maniple, originally used as a pocket-handkerchief, the cords with which our Saviour was bound and led away to Caiaphas; and now you wish me to take our Saviour's words literally and materially. His words, however, are spirit, and they are life. And in this case, when He said, "This is my body which is given for you" (S. Luke xxii. 19), it is very plain that He could not mean them, and that His disciples could not take them—literally; for that bread could not be His Body, except in thought, neither could it be the "body that was given," for it was not yet "given" for the salvation of the world, except prospectively in the counsel of GOD. Neither could the wine they drank visibly be His Blood, that was not yet shed.

And, as proof that, after the Lord had said, "Drink ye all of this," the wine still continued the same in substance, Clement of Alex. (Pædag., etc., b. ii. c. ii. p. 158) remarks, ὅτι δὲ οἶνος ἦν τὸ εὐλογηθὲν ἀπέδειξε πρὸς τοὺς μαθητὰς λέγων· οὐ μὴ πίω ἐκ τοῦ γεννήματος τῆς ἀμπέλου ταύτης, that the Saviour spake of it as of "this fruit of the vine," inasmuch as the elements after the consecration do not change their nature, οὐδὲ γὰρ μετὰ τὸν ἁγιασμὸν τὰ μυστικὰ σύμβολα τῆς οἰκείας ἐξίσταται φύσεως, says Theodoret (Evan. Dial. II.) ; "but they are reckoned and worshipped for that which they are believed to be." The doctrine of the Church of England, says Bishop Jeremy Taylor (Real Pres. sect. i. 4), being that "after the minister of the holy mysteries has ritely prayed, and blessed, and consecrated the bread and wine, the symbols become changed into the body and blood of Christ after a sacramental, that is, in a spiritual real manner; so that all that worthily communicate do by faith receive Christ really, effectually, to all the purposes of His passion."

It is therefore difficult to believe that the disciples, so far as they understood their Master's words, did take them otherwise than figuratively, as they often had taken them before. For instance, when our Saviour said to Peter, "Thou art Satan," and also, "Thou art a stone or rock," which is the intended meaning of "Peter" in S. Matt. xvi. 18; or when our Saviour said, "I am the door," "I am the true vine," "I am the living bread;" or when the prophet spake of Him as of "the Sun of righteousness," of "the Day Star," or when He is alluded to as "the Lion of Judah," &c.—all these and like expressions were figurative. And, since the very words of our Saviour when He instituted the sacrament of His Body and Blood could not be taken as literally true in a material sense, but were prospectively true in a spiritual one, it is not easy to see by what means they should be taken literally and materially ever after.

But such questions appear to me irrelevant, and entirely out of keeping with the dignity and unsearchable nature of this "most Holy Mystery," thus called by the Church, because, says Bishop Jeremy Taylor, "it is a sacrament and a mystery," "a thing which by nature is an undiscernible

III.—*The Mystery of the Holy Eucharist.*

secret," "which is impossible to be understood, and therefore is not fit to be inquired after" (Real Pres. sect. i. 2). It is a mystery which, believe me, neither you nor I, nor any of your friends, whatever they may say, can possibly understand. Therefore do not feel dissatisfied with the English Church for an imaginary reason of this kind; the less so as "the manner," says Jeremy Taylor, "was defined but very lately; there is no need at all to dispute it; no advantages by it, and therefore it were better it were left at liberty to every man to think as he please; for there was peace in the Church for <u>a thousand years</u>, while they were satisfied with believing heartily without inquiring curiously." For, in sooth, "if men would but do reason, there were in all religion no article which might more easily excuse us from meddling with questions about it than this of the Holy Sacrament (*ibid.* i. 2, 4). As I wish to "do reason," agreeing as I do with Bishop Taylor on the subject, you will, I hope, excuse me if I decline to carry the discussion of it any further.

Ritualist. Well, but, even upon your own showing, as we cannot pay too great honour to the Holy Sacrament, so also may we not celebrate it with too much pomp.

Catholic. Indeed, we may, for it depends entirely on the view we take of it. Compare, if you please, the lone simplicity of the Last Supper, and the garments worn by the Lord Himself and His Apostles destined to sit with Him upon thrones in the kingdom of heaven, with the pomp of the Levitical service and sacrifices that were shadows of the Sacrifice figured at that same Supper and soon after accomplished on the Cross. Surely, if pomp and show were necessary to the due celebration of that Holy Sacrament, our Saviour would have set the example, and His Apostles would have enforced it.

But, on the contrary. While He brought together the riches of all lands for the services of the temple, that were meant as mere shadows of realities to be found in Him alone, He yet Himself appeared in the greatest humility, not at His birth only, not only during His life on earth, but even when He consecrated the symbol of His Blood as of the price paid for the redemption of man, and that of His Body as given for the life of the world. Because the first service was earthly and temporal, the second spiritual and heavenly, the first was of rites and ceremonies, the second was "in spirit and in truth." Therefore were neither rites nor ceremonies, neither pomp nor show prescribed for the latter service, which is spiritual.

For my part, therefore, when, on the one hand, I think of that Last Supper in the upper room at Jerusalem, of the heavy swell of coming agony and of profound grief in my Saviour's breast, of His parting words of comfort to His

III.—*The Mystery of the Holy Eucharist.* 73

sorrowing disciples, and of His earnest prayer to His Father; and when, on the other hand I feel that the only offering I can bring to Him thus suffering for me, is that of a broken and contrite heart, nothing but solemn simplicity seems to me in harmony with those Holy Mysteries. But the pomp, the pageant, and the ceremonies you seem to love so well, look to me like a mockery, if not like a parody of the whole thing, so little do they agree with the still, soft, and soothing influences of the Holy Spirit whom we pray to come down upon us at that solemn hour.

Therefore is it impossible for me to see in your "Ritualism" a proof of real, heartfelt reverence and worship, though it may suit you to give that as the reason. For it seems to me that the nearer we draw in spirit to what did actually take place at the Last Supper, the more simple also will our ritual and service be: becoming, solemn, and in order—but no more. Whereas your ritualistic practices look more like a mimicry of the Levitical service, connected as they seem to be in your mind, with your idea of Sacerdotalism, that pretends to repeat the sacrifice, wrought once, and accomplished for ever, "of the Lamb slain from before the foundation of the world," though you do so against the direct witness of Scripture, that "Christ, after he had offered one sacrifice for sins, for ever, sat down on the right hand of God. For by one offering he hath perfected for ever them that are sanctified" (Heb. x. 12, 14). Thus, then, while you pretend to repeat the sacrifice offered once for ever and for all, do I, with the Holy Apostle, and "as often as I eat this bread and drink this cup," τον θάνατον τοῦ Κυρίου καταγγέλλω, only, proclaim, announce, or "show the Lord's death until he come" (1 Cor. xi. 26).

IV.—OF INCENSE, OF LIGHTS, AND OF THE EUCHARISTIC SACRIFICE.

*ITUALIST.* You then would object to incense at the Holy Eucharist?

Catholic. Assuredly. What need is there of it?

Ritualist. But surely the use of it is of ancient date. "Thuris usus, the use of incense," says Card. Bona, "was a solemn rite among all nations, even barbarous ones;" so that, without incense, "nullum sacrificium rite peragi, crediderint," no sacrifice, in their opinion, could be ritely offered. And the same authority adds (lib. i. c. xxv. s. 9), "thuris usum in sacrificio ab *apostolica* descendisse traditione, idque *legis Mosaicæ* exemplo," that the use of incense at the sacrifice of the Mass came down through tradition from the Apostles, and this, too, after the example of the Mosaic ritual.

Catholic. I thought so. The use of incense, or of some mixed spices at sacrifices, is, we know, ancient; it was prescribed in the Tabernacle, and seems to have been admitted thence into the Christian Church at an early date, though we have no proof of it before the middle of the fourth century. Θυμίαμα is, indeed, mentioned in the second Canon, so called, of the Apostles; but, whatever authority be granted to it in the Greek Church, that of Rome does not reckon very highly this "sic dictus Canon Apostolicus," as Card. Bona calls it. In vain, however, do I look for example or for authority to use incense, either in the New Testament or in the early Church.

Ritualist. But did not the wise men offer incense to our Saviour ὡς Θεῷ, as unto GOD?

Catholic. That was λίβανος, not your θυμίαμα. You would not, however, quote that as a precedent for the use of incense at the Holy Eucharist, especially as some of the later authorities warn you that those offerings were intended to teach us to offer unto GOD ὡς χρυσὸν τὴν πίστιν, ὡς δὲ λίβανον τὰς πράξεις, ὡς δὲ σμύρναν τὴν τοῦ σώματος νέκρωσιν, "faith for gold, our works for incense, and the mortification of the body for myrrh" (Theophan. Hom. xiv. in Suicer. s. v.)

Ritualist. Yet do we not read, in the book of Revelation, of the elders, and of the angel with a golden censer with much incense?

Catholic. We read there of θυμίαμα, which is not "incense," since, in Rev. xviii. 13, it is there used with λίβανος, "incense" properly so called, or "frank-incense," mentioned here only and in

S. Matt. ii. 11, in the New Testament. Let it be incense, that is, perfume, however, for the sake of argument, would you dare act here upon earth things done in heaven? If so, and supposing you could do it without profaneness, or, at least, without an amount of presumption from which one's feelings of reverence and one's sober sense recoil, you should be consistent and wear a crown, carry palms in your hands, play upon the harp, and, assuredly, be clad in white, and not in coloured garments. Yet it is very possible that indiscretion may have gone so far as to borrow the use of incense from the Apocalypse; since "forte patres nostri," says the learned Augustine, "hunc morem ex *Apocalypsi* didicerunt" (De Sacr. Vas. p. 221); may be our fathers learnt the use of incense from the Apocalypse, ch. viii. 3. I do not know whether the practice be mentioned earlier than the fourth century, as it is by S. Ephraem, in his testament (Syr. Lat. ed. Assem. S. Ephr. Opp. Græc. L. vol. ii. p. 399; S. Ephræmi S. Op. Selecta. Overbeck, p. 143, et Græc. L. vol. ii. p. 237), μήτε μὴν ἀρώμασί με ἐνταφιάσατε —ἀλλὰ δότε ἀτμίδα καπνισμοῦ εὐωδίας ἐν οἴκῳ Θεοῦ, καπνίσατε δὲ ὑμῶν τὰ θυμιάματα ἐν οἴκῳ Θεοῦ. I can, however, find no trace whatever of it in the Apostolic Fathers, after whose time I question if any ceremonies practised in the Church can fairly be called "Catholic and Apostolic," since they then began, more or less, to differ in different countries. Even the most ancient liturgies we have, are no safe guides on the subject; as their interpolations, additions, and alterations from time to time are a notorious fact.

On the contrary, such a passage as this from Justin Martyr—"We are no Atheists for worshipping the Maker of the universe, ἀνενδεῆ αἱμάτων καὶ σπονδῶν καὶ θυμιαμάτων, ὡς ἐδιδάχθημεν, λέγοντες, λόγῳ εὐχῆς καὶ εὐχαριστίας ἐφ' οἷς προσφερόμεθα πᾶσιν, ὅση δύναμις αἰνοῦντες, saying, as we have been taught, that He needs neither the blood of victims, libations, nor incense, but praising Him as we do, after our power, with words of prayers and thanksgivings ("verbo enim sacrificari oportet DEO," Lact. D. I. vi. 25), "at all our oblations" (Pro Christ. Apol. II. p. 60)—seems to prove satisfactorily that incense was not then used in the Christian Church; for, had it been in use, Justin Martyr could not have written in this wise. Neither would S. Clement Al. express himself thus: "We must, then, offer unto God, not splendid and sumptuous sacrifices, but θεοφιλεῖς, such as He likes; καὶ τὸ θυμίαμα ἐκεῖνο τὸ σύνθετον τὸ ἐν τῷ νόμῳ, τὸ ἐκ πολλῶν γλωσσῶν τε καὶ φωνῶν, κατὰ τὴν εὐχὴν συγκείμενον, and for the mixed incense mentioned in the Law, raise unto Him in prayer the voices of the multitude praising him in concord" (Strom. vii. p. 719), if he had been in favour of incense.

Ritualist. But we saw just now that incense formed part of the ceremonies connected with sacrifices, whether heathen or Jewish.

Catholic. No doubt; but I do not see what that has to do with the use of it at the Lord's Supper. (1) I cannot find that it formed part of that sacrament, either when first instituted by our Lord Himself or when administered by the Holy Apostles during their lifetime; and (2) I have yet to learn that the Holy Eucharist is a *sacrifice* in the Levitical and sacerdotal sense.

But even then, prayer is the incense God requires, witness David (Ps. cxli. 2), "Let my prayer come before thee as incense, and the lifting up of my hands, as the evening sacrifice." For, as regards the legal incense itself alone, Elias Cretensis (Comm. in Greg. Naz. Or. I. p. 198), who refers the four ingredients that made up the θυμίαμα, to the constitution of Christ's Nature, quotes Isaiah to show that incense under the law, "was an abomination to God." So that, unless you aim at continuing a symbolism which hardly two persons explain alike—some referring it to holiness, and others only to the smell of burnt sacrifices, as does Maimonides, who, with other Rabbis, makes it to consist of eleven spices, one of which, however, was known of only one family—a symbolism which, if it referred, under the law, to Christ, now no longer exists—you see that you cannot use incense as a sacrificial rite only, and that if you use it symbolically, you must first settle what the ingredients were; and, secondly, what is the symbolism they were intended to represent.

Ritualist. If so with incense, what would you say to lights on the altar by day?

Catholic. I would refer you to S. Jerome, who, writing to Vigilantius, scorns, as a calumny, such an imputation; lighting them only at the Gospel.

Ritualist. But Paulinus, who wrote a little before, speaks of lights burning night and day.

Catholic. Whereby he shows, at all events, that the custom was not "Catholic," but local, even in his day.

Ritualist. But did not the Western Church receive it from the Eastern, that had borrowed it from the Mosaic ritual?

Catholic. S. Ephraem did not think so; for he says expressly, in Exod. xxxvii., that, when the daylight shone forth in the person of our Lord, the use and service of lamps lighted before the veil was done away. Nay, the origin of your lights, that burn dim by day, as if to bear witness to the absurdity of lighting them to the sun, may possibly be found in the underground services in catacombs, where incense or other spices were burnt on account of the foul air of such places. But I cannot tarry by this at present, beyond reminding you of what Eusebius says of the Emperor Constantine (lib. iv. c. xxii.)—that he lighted enormous wax tapers, yet only by night, on Easter Eve, in order to bring heathens to the Christian Faith; a display of lights being a heathen custom.

Ritualist. Well, but at all events, there must

have been lights at the Last Supper; for "it was night" when Judas Iscariot went out.

Catholic. Then, celebrate the Holy Eucharist at night; your lights will then be appropriate. Yet, even then, they should not be placed upon the Altar or Table: for, as it seems evident from S. Matt. xxvi. 23; S. John xiii. 20, 25, that the Last Supper was served in the Eastern, and not in the Roman, fashion—our Lord and His disciples sitting on mats spread on the ground, around a small table upon which "the dish" was placed, into which every one dipped his sop—the light, or the lights—lamps and not tapers—must have been either on a lamp-stand outside the circle of those that sat at meat, or on ledges against the wall. So that your friends are correct in saying, " Si autem velint adversarii, lumina antiquitus *in ipso altari* non fuisse collocata, nos omninò consentientes habebunt"—we agree entirely with those who say that, at all events, lights should not be placed upon the altar" (A. K. De Sacr. Vas. p. 218).

Ritualist. Well, but we light our lights, as an emblem of Christ being the Light of the World.

Catholic. By night, they would have a meaning; but, by day, they burn dim to the sun;—a poor emblem, you must own, and with nothing to recommend it; since Christ is "the Light and the Life," as being "the Sun of Righteousness, with healing in his wings." Your lights would do in catacombs; but lighting them to the sun himself, is childish, and looks like a mockery.

No incense then, nor lights are needed for the Eucharist, which is no Levitical sacrifice. "This do in remembrance of me," τοῦτο ποιεῖτε εἰς τὴν ἐμὴν ἀνάμνησιν (S. Luke xxii. 19), said our Lord to His disciples; upon which S. Chrysostom remarks that, as the Passover was in remembrance of the deliverance of Israel from Egypt, so also was the Lord's Supper instituted in remembrance of our deliverance from sin through Him. He, therefore, calls it (ad Hebr. Hom. xvii. 3) ἀνάμνησιν θυσίας—οὐκ ἄλλην θυσίαν, καθάπερ ὁ ἀρχιερεὺς τότε, ἀλλὰ τὴν αὐτὴν ἀεὶ ποιοῦμεν, μᾶλλον δὲ ἀνάμνησιν ἐργαζόμεθα θυσίας. "We do not offer a sacrifice always repeated, like the high priest of old, but we always offer the same, or, rather, we celebrate the commemoration or remembrance of that sacrifice."

Ritualist. You see, ἐργαζόμεθα, "we work out," "we make."

Catholic. No more than our Saviour's words, τοῦτο ποιεῖτε, "Do this."

Ritualist. Ποιεῖτε, here, means a great deal more.

Catholic. Does it? What then?

Ritualist. It means—it means——

Catholic. It means this: ΣΩ. Εἰ δὲ ποιεῖν, οὐ καὶ ἐργάζεσθαί τι; ΙΠ. Ναί.

Ritualist. Well, exactly; "to make," "to work out," "to——"

IV.—Of the Eucharistic Sacrifice.

Catholic. ΣΩ. Ἆρ οὖν οὐ ποιεῖν τί ἐστι τὸ θεῖν; Is not "to run," then, "to make," or "to do" somewhat? ΙΠ. Ποιεῖν μὲν οὖν. By all means—to " make," should you say, or to " do"?

Ritualist. To " do," of course.

Catholic. ΣΩ. Ὁ κακῶς ἄρα θέων κακὸν καὶ αἰσχρὸν ἐν δρόμῳ τοῦτο ἐργάζεται. So, then, he who runs badly " does," or " makes" this in his race? (Hip. Min. p. 20, ed. L.)

Ritualist. " Does," of course.

Catholic. So, also, when our Saviour said τοῦτο ποιεῖτε, He did not say, " Make this," as you would have us believe, but, "Do this;" do as I have just done; and take, eat my Body "which is [already] given " (S. Luke xxii. 19) or [already] " broken " (1 Cor. xi. 24) "for you." "Given" and "broken," by the Lord Himself from everlasting, and not by you at the time.

You do not, I trust, imagine that the Lord's Supper is the antitype of the lamb sacrificed daily, morning and evening, in the Temple. Even if it were so, you would have to show (1) the sense, (2) the logic, and (3) the right of giving up the reality of one rite, that of slaying the live lamb, and the shedding of his blood, while you literally retain other ceremonies, such as burning incense, lighting lights, &c. If you wish to be consistent, you must either retain the whole, or give up the whole. But that you cannot retain it, and must give it up, as "old and done away," the Apostle teaches you in the Ep. to the Hebrews (ch. vii. 12); showing that "the priesthood being changed, there is made of necessity a change of the law." For that "the law, having a shadow of good things to come, and not the very image of the things, can never make the comers thereunto perfect"—"the body of those shadows being of Christ," as S. Paul says elsewhere.

Those rites and ceremonies, then, being the mere shadow of the reality that is in Christ, I cannot see how any one can consistently, that is, sensibly, pretend (1) to continue the shadows while professing to embrace the reality, and (2) to retain the symbols only of some of those shadows while he perpetuates others in their original outline. Surely, when the sun is risen, even the morning star, harbinger of his coming, is lost in the brightness of his beams, and ceases to shine. Now that the Sun of Righteousness has risen and shines upon us, what need have we of the stars that shone in the night before His appearing? Therefore do we find that as complete a change took place at His coming as ever we see at sunrise; so complete, indeed, from the shadows of the law to realities found in Him, that He who is consecrated our High Priest for evermore, though of the tribe of Judah and not of that of Levi, never once went into the sanctuary while He was on earth, not being priest according to the Levitical priesthood; neither did He ever offer a sacrifice, not being Himself a Levite; "for," says the Apostle (Heb. viii. 4), "if

He were on earth He should not be a Priest; seeing that they are Priests that offer gifts according to the Law." But He waited until He made His one entrance into the Holiest abode of His eternal Priesthood in the heavens.

Bear in mind, then, that the Holy Eucharist is not a commemoration of that daily sacrifice, but of the lamb slain once a year, and that, too, by every Israelite, at the Passover. It was thus slain and eaten by every man for himself, in token—if types mean anything—not only (1) of "the chosen generation and royal priesthood" of "those who are to be priests unto GOD and Christ," Who, in this sense, is "their High Priest for evermore;" but also (2) of the passing character of the Levitical priesthood, as a service of types and shadows. And especially, (3) of the death of the Lamb, that could take place, and that did take place only once; after which followed the feast on his flesh, (*a*) as food and sustenance for every Israelite, and (*b*) in token as well as in remembrance of that death,—but assuredly, not in repetition of it; for the same lamb could only be slain once. Yea, even when afterwards GOD ordained the priesthood, and that the rites and ceremonies relating thereto should be performed daily, but especially at "the Feast" of the Passover, the people did not therefore give up slaying and eating the paschal lamb, every man for himself; since it was at such a supper that the Lamb of GOD Himself taught His disciples the mystical union that was henceforth to bind Him to them through the spiritual eating and drinking of His Body and Blood, under the form of Bread and Wine which Himself consecrated; and that was to be the bond of the closest and holiest communion of every member, not only with Him, the Head, but also one with another, in Him and through Him. So that, in fulfilment thereof, as the death and sacrifice of the Son of Man could only happen once, and did so take place, we now keep the feast of His Body and Blood, in remembrance—but not in repetition—of His death and passion until He come.

And so little did the Lord mean this sacrament to be an "actual sacrifice" in the Levitical sense, to be performed with all the sacerdotal pomp of the Levitical service, that neither He nor His Apostles ever once alluded to it by that name. So little, also, did He mean His disciples to take His words literally and materially, so as to believe they did actually eat His flesh and drink His blood, and so fully did He thereby only mean the mystical union He is pleased to allow between Himself and His faithful disciple in the Lord's Supper in the idea of πνευματικὴ τροφή, spiritual food and sustenance, as Origen calls it (Hom. xviii. in Jerem. p. 178, ed. H.), through His spiritual and not His material presence in that sacrament—that He says of Himself, "I am the bread of GOD; the bread of life: He that cometh to me shall never hunger; and he that believeth

IV.—Of the Eucharistic Sacrifice.

on me shall never thirst." "I am the living bread which came down from heaven: if any man eat of this bread, he shall live for ever: and the bread that I will give is my flesh, which I will give for the life of the world." Whereon I may remark that neither the Greek nor the English gives an adequate and full sense of our Saviour's words. He spake them in Syriac, and in that language the same word means "flesh" and "bread," thus combining the idea of "support and nourishment," while the Greek for "bread" also means "a loaf," of which many partake around the same table; thus imparting the idea of union and fellowship that "bread" does not give. So that our Saviour did not say "my flesh," but "my body, which I will give for the life of the world:" and thus wherever "flesh" occurs in S. John vi.; the comparison being fuller and the harmony far greater between "body" and "a loaf" than between "flesh" and "bread." But especially, does this bear on the idea of *communion*, μετάληψις and μετοχή, not only with Him whose Body is broken, but also one with another around His table; in one sense, the "Communion of saints," the partaking together all over the world of the same Body, and sharing the same loaf.

Ritualist. A grand idea, that of the CATHOLIC EUCHARISTIC SACRIFICE.

Catholic. Grand indeed, if it were true; but your idea of it is a dream. As in the Holy Catholic Church, nothing is "Catholic"—that is, "one and the same and universal," but the foundation upon which the building rests, namely, FAITH IN CHRIST; so also in this "Catholic Eucharistic Sacrifice," that sounds so well, nothing is "Catholic" but THE SPIRIT, through which every "faithful" partakes of these Holy Mysteries according to his proportion of faith in them—and not else. For, as regards the form, we have seen (1) that neither the vestments nor the ceremonies thereof are "Catholic;" (2) we see that it is no "sacrifice" in the Levitical sense; and (3) as to the ritual words in use, all I can say is, that I have examined, it is true, only forty-nine Liturgies of the Church Catholic, but, of these, no two are alike. The only point on which they all agree is—Faith in Christ, who made atonement for the sins of the whole world. To my mind, then, and to that of sober reflection, our Saviour, in a way, prefigured this diversity in words, and this oneness through the Spirit only, when, on the one hand, He said to the Jews, who strove among themselves, saying, "How can this man give us his flesh (his body) to eat?" and, on the other hand, to some of His disciples who were offended at it and said, "This is an hard saying; who can hear it?"—"It is the Spirit that quickeneth; the flesh profiteth nothing: the words that I speak unto you, they are spirit, and they are life" (S. John vi.).

In all this I see no actual *sacrifice*, that is, no repetition, material and visible, though haply under another form, of the slaying of the Paschal lamb.

But I do see the fulfilment of types and shadows of Him who is that Lamb slain, also at the Passover, and once for all—for Christ "died unto sin once," "and now dieth no more"—whose Body after the death and sacrifice of Himself on the Cross, serves as spiritual food and sustenance for His people; and who is thus both the Lamb of GOD, without spot or blemish, "that was slain from the foundation of the world," and "the life," "the bread of heaven" and "of life," all of which are to be understood typically and spiritually, like everything else that concerns our mystical and mysterious union with Him who is Spirit, and our life through Him who is the Bread of heaven. If, therefore, His words, "I am the living bread which came down from heaven," "I am the bread of GOD," "I am the bread of life," must, of necessity, be taken figuratively and spiritually, I do not see by what process of analogous reasoning, when He says, "This is my body," these words are to be taken in any other sense than that of spiritual food. Further, I maintain that to invest this Holy Sacrament with anything material and gross is not reverence, but a mockery; is not the worship of Him "in spirit and in truth," but it is a vulgar and sensual adoration of matter: it is not faith, but superstition; not a spiritual worship, but idolatry.

Ritualist. Would you, then, have every man celebrate the Holy Eucharist for himself, as the Israelites did the Passover?

Catholic. What do you mean? Among other positive proofs that the service of the Eucharist and that the Communion therein enjoyed are both purely spiritual is (1) that, as our Saviour instituted this sacrament in remembrance of Himself, and told His Apostles to do it in memory of Him; and as they both continued to do so and delivered it unto the bishops and priests they ordained, the elements of Bread and Wine may not minister the graces of the Spirit they are intended to impart "to the faithful" only, without this consecration—that would not be necessary if the spiritual service of this Sacrament were in any way like that of the Levitical Passover. And (2) not only does θυσία, even where rendered "sacrifice," not necessarily imply actual slaughter—as, *e.g.*, in our offering "our bodies a living sacrifice," whereby is meant a thing, or action, or life, *made sacred* by being consecrated to GOD— but, as the Lord's Supper is nowhere in the New Testament alluded to as θυσία, "sacrifice," nor yet in any of the Apostolic Fathers, so also did the Apostles, and the bishops and priests they ordained, as being ministers of a new covenant, of a spiritual service with spiritual sacrifices, never arrogate to themselves the title of ἱερεύς, *sacerdos*, in the sense of "priest of the altar" under the Levitical priesthood, as if they were invested with like functions and prerogatives.

Ritualist. In what sense, then, do you understand "the Eucharistic sacrifice?"

IV.—Of the Eucharistic Sacrifice.

Catholic. I understand "sacrifice" in this case, as offered by the Christian priest or presbyter, to mean a service or offering, a rite, sacrament or worship, *made sacred* by being dedicated and offered to GOD; but assuredly not a repetition of the sacrifice of Christ. For even Porphyry (De Abst. lib. ii. 5) tells us that the first θυσίαι, sacrifices or offerings, were the herbs of the field; that θυμιάματα were the smoke of the same when consumed, and that ἀρώματα were so called from ἀρᾶσθαι, being execrations on those who first introduced animal sacrifices. Wherefore ἡμεῖς ὡς τὴν ὑστέραν πλημμέλειαν σημαίνοντα οὐκ ὀρθῶς ἐξακούομεν, τὴν διὰ τῶν ζώων δοκοῦσαν θεραπείαν καλοῦντες θυσίαν, "are we wrong in calling θυσία the service of animal sacrifices, as applied to a later transgression,"—inasmuch as Cain offered unto GOD of the fruits of the earth, θυσίαν τῷ Θεῷ (Gen. iv. 3), and the first-fruits and frankincense were also θυσία, an offering, (Lev. ii. 14), while θυσία was also said of fine flour (*ibid.* v. 11, 12, vi. 15), of the same baked with oil (*ibid.* 21, ed.), of wheat (1 Chron. xxi. 23), of the lifting up of the hands (Ps. cxli. 2); and of praise (Heb. xiii. 13, etc.)

And I take "Eucharistic" to mean "of thanks" or of "thanksgivings," according to the sense given to it by Justin Martyr and by the Apostolic Fathers; a service in which "we praise, we bless, we worship, we glorify, we give God thanks for His great glory." (Comm. Serv. Doxol.) Thus did S. Ignatius write to the Ephesians—συνέρχεσθαι εἰς εὐχαριστίαν Θεοῦ καὶ εἰς δόξαν (ad Eph. 13), "to gather together oftener for the Eucharist, or thankoffering to GOD, and for His praise." Again, σπουδάσατε μιᾷ εὐχαριστίᾳ χρῆσθαι — "give diligence to make use of one Eucharist" (ad Philad. 4, ad Smyrn. 6 and 8), called εὐχαριστία, Justin Martyr tells us, by reason of the προεστὼς τῶν ἀδελφῶν, President of the brethren, who, taking the Bread and Wine mixed with water (κρᾶμα) αἶνον καὶ δόξαν τῷ πατρὶ τῶν ὅλων διὰ τοῦ ὀνόματος τοῦ υἱοῦ καὶ τοῦ πνεύματος τοῦ ἁγίου, ἀναπέμπει, καὶ εὐχαριστίαν ὑπὲρ τοῦ καταξιῶσθαι τούτων παρ' αὐτοῦ ἐπιπολὺ ποιεῖται—"sends forth praise and glory to the Father of all things in the name of the Son and of the Holy Ghost, and gives thanks abundantly for being by Him deemed worthy of this blessing" (J. M. Apol. ii. 97). And again, "GOD says, τὰς εὐχὰς αὐτῶν θυσίας καλεῖν, that He calls their prayers oblations (or sacrifices)." Ὅτι μὲν οὖν καὶ εὐχαὶ καὶ εὐχαριστίαι ὑπὸ τῶν ἀξίων γινόμεναι τέλειαι μόναι καὶ εὐάρεστοί εἰσι τῷ Θεῷ θυσίαι, καὶ αὐτός φημι—" I therefore declare that the prayers and the 'thank-offerings,' or Eucharists, offered unto GOD by those who are worthy of it, are the only oblations (or sacrifices) that are both perfect and acceptable unto GOD" (Justin M. Dial. c. Tryph. p. 344, *et seq.*) Αὐτίκα θυσίαι μὲν αὐτῷ εὐχαί τε καὶ αἶνοι, "prayers and praises, then, are the sacrifices or oblations that please

Him best," says S. Clement Al. (Strom. lib. vii. p. 728). Thus, too, is the Eucharist mentioned in ἐν τῇ ἐκκλησίᾳ παρεχώρησεν ὁ Ἀνίκητος τὴν εὐχαριστίαν τῷ Πολυκάρπῳ—"Anicetus, while in the Church, yielded (the consecration of) the Eucharist to Polycarp" (Concil. Lugd. Reliq. Sacr. Routh. vol. i. p. 393). Even later, S. Cyril of Jerusalem, speaking of the Eucharist, Εὐχαριστία, as of a πνευματικὴ θυσία, of a spiritual (sacrifice or) oblation, ascribes, as we saw, the whole merit of it to the efficacy of the Holy Ghost, saying that πάντως γὰρ οὗ ἐὰν ἐφάψαιτο τὸ Ἅγιον Πνεῦμα, τοῦτο ἡγίασται καὶ μεταβέβληται, "whatsoever the Holy Ghost reaches is both sanctified and transformed" (Catech. Mystag. v.).

This is agreeable to Scripture, to truth, and to the Anglican Church, whose faithful sons hold the Catholic doctrine that the Eucharist is a service of thanksgivings, a sacrament instituted, administered, and taken "in remembrance of our Saviour's death and passion, wherein He offered Himself in sacrifice, and made, once for all, a full, perfect, and sufficient sacrifice, oblation, and satisfaction, for the sins of the whole world,"—ἅπαξ προσηνέχθη καὶ εἰς τὸ ἀεὶ ἤρκεσε, "who was once offered," says S. Chrysostom, "and made satisfaction for ever" (Hom. xvii. in Hebr.). In the words of Justin Martyr, "we do not bring sacrifices and oblations of blood and other libations to the altar," ἀλλὰ ἀληθινοὺς καὶ πνευματικοὺς αἴνους καὶ εὐχαριστίας, "but real and spiritual praises and thanksgivings (Eucharists)," τὴν ἀρίστην καὶ ἁγιωτάτην θυσίαν, "the best and most sacred offering," as S. Clement Al. says of praises and thanksgivings (Strom. viii. p. 717), καὶ οὐ μάτην ἡμεῖς εἰς τοῦτον πεπιστεύκαμεν, οὐδ' ἐπλανήθημεν ὑπὸ τῶν οὕτως διδαξάντων; and our faith in this is not vain, neither have we been led astray by those who taught us thus to believe" (Dial. c. Tryph. p. 346). "Verbo enim sacrificari oportet Deo," "Therefore must we offer unto GOD our sacrifice in words," says Lactantius ("the calves of our lips," "the sacrifice of praise and thanksgivings," &c.), since GOD is the Word, as He declares it. "Summis igitur colendi DEI ritus est, ex ore justi hominis ad DEUM directa laudatio—the highest rite in the worship of GOD, then, is praise offered unto Him straight from the mouth of a just man, that is acceptable unto Him when sent up from a humble heart, with fear and devotion."

We need not, therefore, embrace as "Catholic doctrine" what Theophylact said a thousand years after Justin Martyr, when the Church had sought and already found many inventions in departing from her primitive and simple faith, αὐτὸ τὸ σῶμα τοῦ Κυρίου ἐστὶν ὁ ἄρτος ὁ ἁγιαζόμενος ἐν τῷ θυσιαστηρίῳ, καὶ οὐχὶ ἀντίτυπον; "the bread that is on the altar is the very Body of the Lord, and not a figure —because we are weak and could not eat κρέας ὠμόν, raw meat and man's flesh, therefore does it appear to us bread, but in reality it is flesh." This, however, is of a piece with what follows; namely, "that our Saviour did not say 'Eat ye all of it,' but only 'Drink ye all of it,' because of Judas Iscariot, who took the bread, but hid it, and did not eat it, in order to show the Jews what the Lord had said was His Body; but that he, however, drank of the cup, though unwillingly, unable as he was to hide it. Unless, indeed, it mean mystically that bread, being the more solid food of the two, is not for all, but only for the more perfect; but that the cup, being lighter food, is for all" (Theophyl. ad Matt. c. xxvii.).

Ritualist. But we mix water with the wine in the Holy Sacrament. What say ye to that?

Catholic. Simply that ye have no warrant for it whatever. It is true that, as we saw, Justin Martyr says that τὸ κρᾶμα, the wine and water, was brought τῷ προεστῶτι, to the President of the brethren, for consecration; but as there is no trace of this mixture in our Lord's institution of that sacrament, we may doubtless refer the origin of that custom to the Water and Blood that flowed from His side. It is worthy of notice that the third Canon of the Apostles, which is of Apostolic authority in the Greek Church, forbids to bring to the altar anything παρὰ τὴν τοῦ Κυρίου διάταξιν, "besides what the Lord instituted;" with which agree the words of S. Ambrose: "Indignum dicit Apostolus, esse Domino qui aliter mysterium celebrat, quam ab eo traditum est, non enim potest devotus esse, qui aliter præsumit quam datum est ab authore" (in 1 Cor. xi.). The Greek Canon, however, is explained in the popular commentary, to mean ἄρτος καὶ οἶνος, ἐσμιγμένος μὲ τὸ νερόν, "bread and wine mixed with water;" as told on the authority of S. James, in his Liturgy (p. 62, ed. Neale), where the priest, taking the cup, says: ὡσαύτως μετὰ τὸ δειπνῆσαι, λαβὼν τὸ ποτήριον καὶ κέρασας ἐξ οἴνου καὶ ὕδατος, καὶ ἀναβλέψας εἰς τὸν οὐρανὸν, etc., attributed to our Saviour. But this savours of the later interpolations in all the ancient liturgies, of which Renaudot speaks, and which are notorious; for instance, S. James's Liturgy, in Greek, mentions this κρᾶμα; but the same Liturgy in Syriac (Ren. ii. 126) omits it, and speaks of wine only. For no mention is made of water in our Saviour's institution of this sacrament.

And he would be a rash, as well as reckless, critic, who would here refer us to Athenæus, Alciphron, Aristophanes, and others, for the Greek custom of mixing the κρᾶμα, "wine and water," at their meals; for it was then called κρᾶμα, and not οἶνος, "wine," which our Saviour expressly styles τὸ γέννημα τῆς ἀμπέλου, "the fruit of the vine." The expression found in the Liturgy of S. James occurs also in that of S. Clement (p. 103, ed. N.), as it does in that of S. Mark (p. 25, ed. N.), and in a Coptic MS. of it I brought from Jerusalem; but it is with this as with other Coptic liturgies—

half of them is written in Greek. Whether in Greek or in any translation thereof, it is impossible to put faith in them, adulterated as the original, or originals, have been from the first, that may date from the third or fourth century, if, indeed, so early. Anyhow, wine and water in the sacrament is not a "Catholic" custom, for the Armenian (Gregorian) Church does not adopt it, and the Abyssinian Church for some time used water only instead of wine, from want of grapes in the country to make wine withal. In the Apostolic Constitutions in Coptic, no mention is made of water, but only of bread and wine, being *p-smot*, the figure or semblance of the Body and Blood of Christ, with milk and honey.—Besides, you must show reason why, if the confusion of the two Sacraments of Water and Blood be lawful in the one instance, it should not be so in the other. Why then, if you mix water with wine in the Lord's Supper, do you not mix wine with the water of Baptism; yea, even though Our Saviour's first miracle in Cana of Galilee, condemn such a confusion in either case?

Likewise, as regards the bread, some, like the Romish and the Armenian Churches, use it unleavened, while the Syrian Church mixes salt and oil with it; and yet not generally, for the Jacobites of Egypt quarrel with those of Syria about the quantity thereof to be used. But how do you mix water with the wine?

Ritualist. With a spoon: three drops only.

Catholic. Here, again, your custom is not "Catholic," for some other Churches mix a third of water either cold or warm; while the Syrian Church (S. Ephraem Op. Syr. Lat. ii. p. 30) uses the spoon as an emblem of the tongs with which the seraph took a live coal from the altar and touched Isaiah's lips; the coal itself being held as an emblem of the Holy Sacrament. But the Liturgy of S. Matthew has a prayer over the spoon, "per quod *lancea crucis* significatur" (Fabr. Cod. N. T. iii. p. 214). So much for "Catholic" symbolism.

But although I cannot expect to have altered your opinion in any way, seeing your mind is made up, yet, from what has been said, do I feel convinced with Bishop Taylor "that the presence of Christ in the sacrament is real and spiritual;" and "that the spiritual is also a real presence, and that they are hugely consistent, is easily credible to them that believe that the gifts of the Holy Ghost are real graces, and a spirit is a proper substance. Therefore, when things spiritual are signified by materials, the thing under the figure is called *true*, and the material part is opposed to it as less true or real" (Real. Pres. sect. i. 5, 6). It is therefore said to be a mystery, and a holy mystery. "Mysterium est," says Bishop Taylor, ἀπόρρητον, καὶ θαυμαστὸν καὶ ἀγνοούμενον, ineffable, wonderful, and unknown, as Joh. Damascenus calls it ('Ιερὰ κατ. c. vi.); and so little understood, spiritual and mysterious as it is, that, with Hooker, "it would be best that men would more give themselves to meditate with silence what we have by the sacrament, and less to dispute of the manner how" (bk. v. ch. 67, 3, *et seq.*) "Faith," says Isaac, Presbyter of Antioch, "beckons to thee to draw near and eat, but in silence, and to drink, but without inquiry" (Assem. Bib. Or. vol. i. p. 220). But it were no mystery if Christ's presence therein were made visible, and it were true that the bread we eat is material flesh under the semblance of bread, and the wine we drink material blood under the semblance of wine, as taught by the Romish Church. Therefore, also, is it no actual sacrifice, αἷμα καὶ σφαγή, no "blood and slaughter," or "blood and victim," as Theophylact would have it; but it is called θυσία, oblation, or sacrifice, in order to specify the kind of oblation Christ made of Himself, once, for ever, and for all.

But rather, and if so be, one may approach to the definition of a mystery which no one can understand, does S. Ephraem say more correctly: "Thy bread hides the spirit which is not eaten, and in Thy wine burns the fire that is not drunk. The Spirit and the fire are two singular wonders that are perceived by our soul only" (S. Ephr. Serm. de Fide X. et Assem. Bib. Or. vol. i. p. 101); and as S. Macarius (Homil. xxvii. p. 386) says plainly, that in the Church are offered the Bread and the Wine, as ἀντίτυπον τῆς σαρκὸς αὐτοῦ καὶ τοῦ αἵματος, "as symbols of His Body and Blood;"

and they that partake ἐκ τοῦ φαινομένου ἄρτου, πνευματικῶς τὴν σάρκα τοῦ κυρίου ἐσθίουσι, "of the bread as it appears, spiritually eat the flesh of the Lord." So that as the term θυσία, "sacrifice," is used for this spiritual service only in commemoration of the sacrifice of Christ before accomplished, and is no more to be taken literally, as regards the priest who offers it, than the expression θυσία ζῶσα, "the living sacrifice," in which he is told to offer his body unto GOD, which is his reasonable service,—I conclude that he is, and can be, no priest in the Levitical sense, but that he is πρεσβύτερος, a "presbyter," who, according to his Catholic and Apostolic ordination, has the power delegated to him, as only "steward of the Mysteries of GOD," to consecrate the elements of bread and wine so as to make them the means of spiritual life and growth, according to Christ's holy institution; and no more. "Wherefore," says S. Clement Al., "do we not sacrifice to GOD, who is in need of nothing—τὸν δ' ὑπὲρ ἡμῶν ἱερευθέντα δοξάζομεν σφᾶς αὐτοὺς, ἱερεύοντες, but we glorify Him who was sacrificed for us, by offering our own selves in sacrifice to Him; for He taketh pleasure in nothing but our salvation" (Strom. vii. p. 707). Πρεσβύτερος — not ἱερεύς—θυσίαν προσφέρεται, says the ancient Church (Can. Ap. 3); the Presbyter, then, brings or offers an oblation, rather than the Priest a sacrifice.

V.—OF THE PRIESTHOOD, AND OF THE VESTMENTS THEREOF.

CATHOLIC. As the term θυσία is not used for the Eucharist in the New Testament, nor in the Apostolic Fathers, so neither does the term ἱερεύς occur in them with reference to the Christian priesthood. S. Clement mentions ἱερεῖς (1 Ep. ad Cor. 25, 32, etc.) in connection with heathen customs and with the Levitical priesthood; and S. Ignatius (Ep. ad Philad. 9) makes use of the expression καλοὶ καὶ οἱ ἱερεῖς· κρεῖσσον δὲ ὁ ἀρχιερεὺς ὁ πεπιστευμένος τὰ ἅγια τῶν ἁγίων, ὃς μόνος πεπίστευται τὰ κρυπτὰ τοῦ Θεοῦ· αὐτὸς ὢν θύρα τοῦ πατρός, δι' ἧς εἰσέρχονται Ἀβραὰμ καὶ Ἰσαὰκ καὶ Ἰακώβ, καὶ οἱ προφῆται, καὶ οἱ ἀπόστολοι καὶ ἡ ἐκκλησία· πάντα ταῦτα εἰς ἑνότητα Θεοῦ, whence it is clearly impossible to affirm that S. Ignatius meant ἱερεῖς of Christian priests of his time, coupled as the term is with ἀρχιερεύς, the high priest, "who is the door of the Father, at which enter Abraham, Isaac,

Jacob, and the prophets, with the Apostles and the Church."

But, rather, seeing, on the one hand, how continually the same Father speaks of the πρεςβύτεροι, "presbyters," and of the "presbytery," as inseparable from the bishop, and, on the other hand, how S. Clement mentions ἱερεῖς καὶ λευῖται πάντες οἱ λειτουργοῦντες τῷ θυσιαστηρίῳ, "the priests and all the Levites who minister at the altar" (*ibid.*, 32), and elsewhere of the office appointed for the high priest, for the priests, for the Levites, and for the laity (*ibid.*, 40), as still existing in his time, it is far more according to reason to take ἱερεύς, "priest," in the same sense when used by S. Ignatius; the more so as, even in the fifth century, λευίτης, "a Levite," was taken in the sense adopted by S. Clement; thus—ὁ δὲ τοιοῦτος, εἴτε λευίτης ἐστὶν, εἴτε πρεσβύτερος, εἴτε ἐπίσκοπος κ.τ.λ. (Synes. Epist. ad Episc. 58). So that the frequent use of the term ἱερεύς in the so-called early liturgies of S. Clement, S. James, S. Matthew, S. Mark, and others, seems sufficient either to ascribe the liturgies themselves—or, at least, these interpolations—to a much later date.

Ritualist. Do I understand you to say that the term ἱερεύς, in the sense of "priest offering a sacrifice," as applied to Christians, was not used in the first century after Christ?

Catholic. It may have been used; but I have not yet seen an instance of it, nor of the term θυσία,

V.—Of the Priesthood.

which is sometimes said of the Eucharist—as, *e.g.*, in the liturgy of S. Clement—taken in the sense of a Levitical sacrifice offered by the priest, ἱερεύς.

The early Church only knew of ἐπίσκοποι, πρεσβύτεροι καὶ διάκονοι, "bishops, presbyters, and deacons." Justin Martyr, indeed, says, οὐ δέχεται δὲ παρ' οὐδενὸς θυσίας ὁ Θεὸς, εἰ μὴ διὰ τῶν ἱερέων αὐτοῦ—"GOD does not accept sacrifices (or oblations) from any one, except through his priests;" but he explains these words, (1) as regards ἱερεῖς here mentioned, by referring it to ἀρχιερατικὸν τὸ ἀληθινὸν γένος ἐσμὲν τοῦ Θεοῦ—"the true race of high priests we are unto GOD," laity as well as clergy; and (2) as regards θυσίας by adding, πάντας οὖν οἱ διὰ τοῦ ὀνόματος τούτου θυσίας, ἃς παρέδωκεν Ἰησοῦς ὁ Χριστὸς γίνεσθαι, τουτ' ἔστιν ἐπὶ τῇ εὐχαριστίᾳ τοῦ ἄρτου καὶ τοῦ ποτηρίου, τὰς ἐν παντὶ τόπῳ τῆς γῆς γινομένας ὑπὸ τῶν Χριστιανῶν, προλαβὼν ὁ Θεὸς, μαρτυρεῖ εὐαρέστους ὑπάρχειν αὐτῷ—"Therefore GOD, anticipating all those who, in the name of Jesus Christ, present unto Him the oblations prescribed and delivered unto us by Christ Himself—that is, the Bread and Wine of the Eucharist, that are offered everywhere by Christians—declares them to be well pleasing unto Him."

Whence it is evident that here θυσία is not "a sacrifice" in the Levitical or sacerdotal sense, but an oblation or offering of thanksgivings, a "thank-offering." So that we may be prepared to find, as we do in the so-called Canons of the Apostles (Can. iii.), that the θυσία of the Eucharist is offered by a πρεσβύτερος, and not by ἱερεύς, a term that is not once named in those Canons. "Ad testimonia Patrum dico," says Card. Bellarmine, "primos Christianos, propter recentem memoriam sacerdotii Aaronici, abstinuisse non solum a vocabulo templi, sed etiam *sacerdotii* ne viderentur adhuc durare Judaicæ cæremoniæ. Itaque Apostoli, in suis Epistolis pro *sacerdotibus*, Episcopos, et Presbyteros, pro templis ecclesias dicunt : et similiter loquuntur Justinus, Ignatius, et cæteri antiquissimi Patres" (De Cultu Sanct. cap. iv. in Suicer. Thes. s. v.) ; words of your own friend, that stamp your "sacerdotalism" of an actual and continually repeated sacrifice, etc., as an innovation.

Ritualist. "My sacerdotalism"—what do you mean by that?

Catholic. I mean "Sacerdotalism and Leviticism," that seems to be your idea, as contrasted with "Christian priesthood," which is mine.

Ritualist. What then?—do you mean about Confession and Absolution?

Catholic. That, and other things besides.

Ritualist. Don't you then believe in the power of the keys?

Catholic. Yes; but it is one of the things I believe without understanding them. I am, of course, ready to grant implicit faith alone, to mysterious matters of faith, unsearchable to the under-

V.—Of the Priesthood.

standing, and taught me in the Word of GOD; but this is more a matter of persuasion than of faith, wherein the understanding should be satisfied by sufficient proofs. I can understand how one gift—say that of loosing and binding on earth—might be perpetuated, while other gifts—such as healing the sick and working miracles—should be discontinued. But as I do not yet quite understand (1) why certain gifts granted to the Apostles should necessarily be imparted to their successors, and as (2) I see that many of those gifts were not imparted either to Timothy or to Titus, and that others granted unreservedly "to believers" in general (S. Mark xvi. 16, 17) have long ceased altogether—while I believe, in deference to my betters, that S. Matth. xvi. 20, xviii. 18; S. John xx. 23, may, in a manner, apply to presbyters also—I yet understand it so little to my own satisfaction, that I should for myself be very wary in the exercise of this power; lest I made a mistake. For in a matter of this kind, the mere opinion of a man, be he who he will, would go for nothing at all, without proofs drawn from Holy Scripture; according to the good advice of S. Cyril of Jerusalem.

Ritualist. What then, would you do in case one of your flock came to you to confess his sins, and to seek absolution?

Catholic. I would not go beyond the words the Church puts in my mouth, and which I, as her servant, am safe in repeating. But I never could bring myself to say, on my own authority, to my fellow-man: I absolve thee; neither can I understand how an honest and sincere man can say so without a twitch of his conscience, crying from within: Sinner, is thine own account settled, that thou shouldest absolve thy brother? So that if that or any other man offered me Absolution I would not accept it; but I would refer him to the tribunal at which he and I shall answer, each of us for himself. For "to my Master" in heaven, not to my fellow-servant on earth, "do I stand or fall."

Ritualist. No!—you are not far advanced then.

Catholic. Quite far enough in this respect. In the case of one coming to me "to open his grief, that by the ministry of GOD'S holy word he may receive the benefit of absolution, together with ghostly counsel and advice," I should encourage him so to do; and, giving him the best advice I could, I should then direct him to "Him who alone hath power to forgive sins," and "who delighteth in showing mercy and pity." This, I should look upon as only a part and duty of my office as priest; thus trying, as S. Paul says, to be "helper of my brother's joy." But there is, I trow, a wide gap between this and what I conceive your idea of the same office to be; at least, judging from the use, or, may be, the abuse, of it, I have seen, that makes Confession compulsory, and Absolution conditional on certain degrees of sin, invented and arranged by man and not by GOD; one man thus enslaving another man under the most tyrannical thraldom, in a way to which no one, who is not weak enough to resign all feeling of personal responsibility, would, for one moment, submit. That is, to me, assuming to be "lords over GOD'S heritage," which S. Peter forbids, and "to have dominion over the faith of the flock," denounced alike by S. Paul and by S. Chrysostom. It is not priesthood, the pattern of which I find in the Good Shepherd, but it is priestcraft; not a trace of which can I find in Holy Scripture; unless, indeed, it originated with "Diotrephes, who loved to have the pre-eminence." It is a net cast over society, with a mesh of it on every family, to be hauled, if it were possible, as of old, by the Inquisition; for the spirit of the whole thing is unchanged, and only waits for an opportunity to work out the same results; it brought many a Christian to the stake, and would do so still, if it could. In short, it takes man from the merciful embrace of his Creator to the merciless judgment of his fellow, no better, and possibly worse than himself; and, practically, it makes man "stand or fall" no longer "to his Master," but to his priest. Nowhere in the Bible do I find anything of the sort. Unless, indeed, you fancy yourself endued with the power of the High Priest of old, and treat your penitent brother as a leper. But, let me tell you, you are the leper yourself, and not the High Priest; and it will be well with you if the touch and intercession of your High Priest and mine be found, at the last, to have cleansed both of us of our leprosy, that "iniquity may not be our ruin;" since even S. Paul feared lest, "after having preached unto others"—he says nothing there about absolving them—"himself should be a castaway."

Ritualist. The Bible, the Bible—rather say—THE CHURCH.

Catholic. I also say "the Church," as well as you; but whereas you see the Bible in the Church, I see the Church in the Bible. A simple conversion of terms, but a very important one, nevertheless.

Seeing, then, the real mind of the early Church on the subject, and applying the term ἱερεύς, *sacerdos*, that gradually came into use, either in general to those that are ἱερωμένοι, in Holy Orders, or in particular to the priest who celebrates the Lord's Supper, we may understand the meaning of S. Chrysostom's words, ὅταν γὰρ ἴδῃς τὸν Κύριον τεθυμένον καὶ κείμενον καὶ τὸν ἱερέα ἐφεστῶτα τῷ θύματι καὶ ἐπερχόμενον, καὶ πάντας ἐκείνῳ τῷ τιμίῳ φοινισσομένους αἵματι, "When thou seest the Lord slain and lying, and the priest standing over the victim and drawing near to it, and all (the assembly) sprinkled with the precious Blood of that victim, thinkest thou thyself still on earth, and not rather in heaven?" &c. Wherein Κύριος τεθυμένος καὶ κείμενος simply states the fact of the θῦμα, of the Lamb often mentioned in the New Testament

V.—Of the Priesthood.

as slain even from the foundation of the world, and as offering a sacrifice of Himself; and does not imply that the θῦμα is wrought by the ἱερεύς at the time; the less so as we are told to contemplate the congregation sprinkled with His Blood—assuredly not literally and visibly—since S. Chrysostom adds, ποιοῦσι δὲ τοῦτο πάντες διὰ τῶν ὀφθαλμῶν τῆς πίστεως, "but all this is done with eyes of faith" (De Sacerd. lib. iii. 4).

And still more to the point: ἓν σῶμά ἐστι καὶ μία θυσία. Ὁ ἀρχιερεὺς ἡμῶν ἐκεῖνός ἐστιν ὁ τὴν θυσίαν τὴν καθαίρουσαν ἡμᾶς προσενεγκών. Ἐκείνην προσφέρομεν καὶ νῦν, τὴν τότε προσενεχθεῖσαν, τὴν ἀνάλωτον. Τοῦτο εἰς ἀνάμνησιν γίνεται τοῦ τότε γενομένου—"The Body is one, and the Sacrifice (or oblation) is one. Our High Priest is He who offers the sacrifice that cleanses us. The one we now offer is that which was then offered, that endures for evermore; and this is done in commemoration of that which was done at that time" (ad Heb. Hom. xvii. 3). Wherein the Greek Church of to-day agrees, when speaking of the ἁγία προσκομιδή of the holy oblation, so called from there being at it bread and wine offered to GOD, εἰς ἀνάμνησιν τοῦ Χριστοῦ, ὅστις, "θυσίαν ἑαυτὸν προσήγαγε τῷ Θεῷ καὶ Πατρὶ διὰ τῆς προσφορᾶς τοῦ Σώματος αὐτοῦ, ὡς Ἀμνὸς θυόμενος, καὶ ὡς Ἀρχιερεύς, καὶ Υἱὸς ἀνθρώπου, προσφέρων καὶ προσφερόμενος, ἅμα δὲ ἱεροθυτούμενος, in "remembrance of Christ, who brought Himself in sacrifice unto GOD the Father, through the oblation of His Body, as the Lamb slain, as the High Priest, and as the Son of Man, offering and being offered, and withal, in sacred oblation" ('Ιερὰ κατήχ. περὶ προσκομ, p. 35); ἱεροθυτούμενος being here in the sense of ἱερόθυτα, offerings sacred to GOD; as ἱεροθυτούμενος καπνός (Aristoph. Av. 1266), that explains, in a degree, the offering and sacrifice of Himself unto GOD, "εἰς ὀσμὴν εὐωδίας, for a sweet-smelling savour."

Ritualist. On these terms, then, what vestments would you grant to the priest?

Catholic. The only vestment given him by the early Church—white, as the fittest and best for a minister of a spiritual service under the New Covenant. "Vestes igitur, gemmas," says Lactantius (Div. Just. lib. vi. c. 25), "et cætera, quæ habentur in pretio, si quis putet DEO cara, is plane, quid sit DEUS, nescit, cui putat voluptati esse eas res, quas etiam homo si contempserit, jure laudabitur—The man who thinks that vestments, precious stones, and other things of the kind called valuable, are agreeable unto GOD, evidently does not know what GOD is; for he imagines that GOD cares for things which men are wise to despise." And S. Seperian, Bishop of Gabala, says, also to the purpose, in his Homily on Baptism, p. 96: "The vestments which GOD commanded Moses to make for Aaron of different materials and colours, and embroidered with gold and precious stones, were so made because of the dulness or grossness of the people, that through this pomp and outward show, they should learn to venerate holy things. But the honour of the priest is not in purple and crimson, in fine linen and in vestments of blue, but it lies in righteousness. Wherefore David says, 'Let thy priests be clothed with righteousness.' For GOD, in order to show that these vestments were not made as being necessary for the Divine service, but only on behalf of the spectators—since He is not in want of such display, but seeks singleness of spirit, and rejoices in purity of heart, which are the regal purple He loves, and the flowers of faith He admires and likes to see outwardly blossoming in virtues—He commanded that, when Aaron went into the holiest of all, he should put off his robes of fine linen, of crimson, purple, and blue, and that he should enter the sanctuary clad in his white tunic alone."

This, as being the symbol of the righteousness of Christ our High Priest stripped of all Levitical vestments, was perpetuated in the early Church as the fittest garment for priests ministering at the Holy Sacrament of the Supper of the Lord; at least, all we know of the first three or four centuries goes to prove that the priests either wore this white garment or their common dress, during Divine service. Even in the days of Sapor, King of Persia, S. Barbasemin, Archbishop of Seleucia, ordered his clergy, who then wore no distinctive dress, to clad themselves in white, in order to be known from the rest, and thus to escape the king's wrath (Assem.

Bib. Or. vol. iv., p. 336). And you, no doubt, remember what Socrates says of the Novatian bishop, Sisinnius, who, when going to pay his respects to Arcadius, was taunted by some of the court and asked why he wore white, and where it was written that bishops should go in white, replied, ὁ δὲ σὺ πρότερον, εἰπὲ ποῦ γέγραπται μέλαιναν ἐσθῆτα φορεῖν τὸν ἐπίσκοπον, Tell me, first, where it is written that a bishop should be dressed in black? (Socrat. Hist. Eccles. lib. iv. c. 22).

Any how, the voice of the early Church has been in favour of the white vestment alone; and this is the one which the national taste and the sober sense of the English Church has adopted, with full right to choose for herself what she likes of such externals, as characteristic of her simple, solemn, and spiritual service. "It is the Church attire," says Hooker (bk. v. c. 29, 5), "which with us for the most part is usual in public prayer; our ecclesiastical laws so appointing, as well as because it hath been of reasonable continuance, and of special choice was taken out of the number of those holy garments which (over and besides their mystical reference) served for 'comeliness' under the law, and is in the number of those ceremonies which may with choice and discretion be used to that purpose in the Church of Christ, as also for that it suiteth so fitly with that lightsome affection of joy wherein GOD delighteth when His saints praise Him; and so lively resembleth the glory of the saints in heaven, together with the beauty wherein angels have appeared unto men, that they which are to appear for men in the presence of GOD as angels, if they were left to their own choice and would choose any, could not easily devise a garment of more decency for such a service."

Ritualist. Well, it is a matter of taste, I suppose.

Catholic. No, indeed; as you see very well. It is rather, and chiefly, a matter of common sense. For, since, owing to the attitude of the Romish Church and to the leanings of you Ritualists, a change in the vestments implies also a change in the doctrine, as we see it to be the case among your friends; therefore is it plain common sense honestly to keep to what is the established and generally received outward badge of Anglican, and not of Romish, doctrine and practices.

So far, English good taste chose the surplice, not only as being the vestment most becoming a priest in his public ministrations, but also as being of the highest antiquity, as having the noblest origin and the only symbolism worth naming, that of the righteousness of our eternal High Priest, and of the innocence and purity He seeks in His servants; and therefore also does English good taste keep to the surplice, as to the vestment characteristic of the National Church service, which, of all other such services in the world, is in itself at once the most decorous, the most simple, and the most dignified. Whereas your vestments, you see, can claim no higher antiquity than the Roman Empire, no other origin than the wardrobe of a Roman citizen; and no other symbolism, some of them, than that of neck and of pocket handkerchiefs, differently explained East and West; while your ceremonies, if the truth were told, might probably for the most part be found to have a Roman beginning, and, from being Roman, to have become Romish, and as such, enviable in your eyes. Yet, do tell me, on what grounds that deserve either earnest consideration or serious thought?

Ritualist. As I said before, our vestments are legal, and are worn at coronations.

Catholic. We settled the practical value of their "legality"—that does not, however, make them either lawful, loyal or expedient; and as to coronations—we do not attend them every Sunday.

Ritualist. Well, then, once for all, your service is too tame for me; I myself like more excitement; and as regards the use of vestments, incense, postures, &c., in public they are necessary in order to keep men together. Did your plain Protestant service ever do it?

Catholic. How, then, did the Church of the first four centuries—THE MOTHER OF US ALL—keep things and men together, without copes and chasubles, incense or maniples, and with only one white vestment, or perhaps even without that? Things in those days were more real, and men were more in earnest; they lived by faith and died for it, and were kept in the life of that faith by other and better means than outward dress; unless, indeed, you think that the love of many waxing cold, is owing to their wearing lighter apparel. Nay, the very men of thirty years ago to whose earnest and real piety we owe much, did infuse more life into us all without either vestments or incense than ever you will with these. You do not wish me to remind you that "the cowl does not make the monk," do you?

Ritualist. But we are the development of those men.

Catholic. Are you? as smoke is of fire, I suppose; the one a comfort, and the other an eye-sore.

Ritualist. You are not complimentary, certainly.

Catholic. No; but I am in earnest; I resent the further disruption of all order and peace you create in the Church, utterly regardless as you are of aught but your own whims. Believe me, you would do more good, and please God far more, if you brought back to the Church a batch of "poor publicans," such as Wesleyans, and other sheep gone astray from her fold, than by widening your phylacteries and lengthening your stoles.

Ritualist. Wesleyans? Oh! But it is no use going on like that. The Church service should be——

Catholic. What now? out with it.

Ritualist. Why—HISTRIONIC, of course.

Catholic. Do I hear right—"histrionic"? The Christian spiritual worship of the Church of Christ "histrionic," as if it consisted in a dumb show, and the congregations were ignorant heathens! This is news to hear in this year of our Lord eighteen hundred and sixty-seven, from men who call themselves members of the English Church. No wonder if you fill your churches with your "Sunday theatricals"—the term is your own, not mine—especially if you tell your congregations that it is "Christian worship." I, too, went with others, on Christmas Eve, to certain churches at Rome, where people almost trod one upon another, to see "histrionic worship;" bishops and archbishops, arrayed in their robes of silver and gold, dandling wax dolls on their knees; to the sound of beautiful music, however, and amid a profusion of lights. I stared, and wondered how that could be called "Christian worship," and I came out thence disgusted and ashamed of myself.

Ritualist. I knew I should astonish you.

Catholic. Astonish? yes! I take you at your word, however; let it be "histrionic," that is, "theatrical." Do you abide by that?

Ritualist. Yes.

Catholic. Well, then, of course, not only does it imply pomp and display, and scenic furniture, but also, and especially, the acting upon a stage of what is not true, by men, ὑποκριταῖς, who wear a mask, a dress not their own, who say what they neither mean nor believe, and pretend to be what they are not. That is "histrionic" worship; is it what you mean?

V.—Of Vestments.

Ritualist. Not altogether.

Catholic. I should hope not. No wonder, however, if you plead for your coloured vestments, καὶ ἡ πορφύρα, καὶ τὰ ἀργυρώματα, ὥς φησιν ὁ κομικὸς, εἰς τοὺς τραγῳδοὺς χρήσιμα, καὶ οὐκ εἰς τὸν βίον. "for purple and for silver stuffs, which, says the Comic writer, are only fit for actors, but are of no use for daily life," as S. Clement Al. reminds you (Strom. ii. p. 201). But as Nestorianism spread in the East through a change of priestly garments, so also does Popery in the West. With S. Clement, therefore, I say, οὐ γὰρ θέμις δολερὰ εἵματα καὶ χρίσματα εἰς τὴν ἀληθείας παρεισιέναι πόλιν—"it is not lawful to bring in treacherous vestments and anointings into the City of Truth" (Strom. ii. 177). You must therefore choose another expression, than "histrionic," or, rather, and better still, give up your extravagant ideas; for a "histrionic" or "theatrical" acting of the Holy Sacrament is nothing less than an insult to the awful solemnity of that holy rite. Only think of what was the Last Supper!

Ritualist. How, then, would you have it?

Catholic. I would have things done "decently and in order; for GOD is not a God of confusion, but of peace, as in all the Churches of the Saints." And since vestments are, as Hooker says, in themselves "indifferent," and important only for what they betoken, while also, none but the Albe or Surplice is "Catholic," and every Church has right to choose her own apparel—if the Bishops do not act in the matter, all the truly Anglican clergy might, at least, agree to wear the surplice, hood and stole that are consecrated by Anglican use, during the whole of the morning service, that should end with "the Prayer for the Church Militant;" preaching in the black gown of their academical degree in the afternoon and evening services.

Ritualist. In that case, would you have an offertory every Sunday?

Catholic. In all churches where it might be done, I should. But, since the Rubric directs that even "one sentence" only be said, at the discretion of the priest, it seems to show that the collecting of alms every Sunday, or when there is no Holy Communion, was not contemplated by those who framed the Rubric; although they certainly seem to have intended that, when there was no Sacrament, the Morning Service should always end with "the Prayer for the Church Militant." Or, failing this, the Bishops in synod assembled might then tell us what vestments to wear, and what to do, all of us alike; for diversity creates division and scandal as you well know; since you already begin to split among yourselves, even in the matter of bowings or noddings, and you confess you are "at sea, after having been moored three hundred years!" Poor men! What more could you say in derision of your "Catholicism?"

I would, therefore, with Hooker, demand that, in the external form of religion, "such things as are apparently, or can be sufficiently proved, effectual and generally fit to set forward godliness may be reverently thought of" (bk. v. p. 38). All of which may be found to a greater degree in the service of the English Church, when duly performed according to the spirit of the Prayer-book, and to the good taste of the nation, than either in the Romish, Greek, Armenian, Syrian, Abyssinian, Coptic, Lutheran, Reformed, Presbyterian, Puritan, or Independent services. Of all those forms of worship, the Anglican alone really tends to edification, by avoiding the theatrical extreme of some of those Churches, and the familiar, dull, irreverent or careless doings of the others.

But, farewell. It is now for you to show that I am wrong and that you are right. You may, of course, abuse me if you like; but abuse is weak; it is only the sting of conscience in a bad cause. Or you may think my ignorance of Ritualistic lore beneath notice; but this would be neither charitable nor condescending on your part. The better and the more manly way, if you are in earnest, would be for you to disprove all my statements, one by one, using the same weapons as myself—the Bible, the early Fathers, and common sense—and thus to show that, since your doings are, as you say, "legal," they are honestly English and not Romish, and thus also loyal to the realm, lawful and tending to the greater good of the national Church.

Had you acted like sensible and earnest men, more anxious to raise the standard of public worship to edification, than to make yourselves conspicuous by your "histrionic" doings, you would have drawn up a summary of the improvements you proposed in vestments, in the order and time of the services, in any thing, in short, that might contribute to the increase of true religion among the people; and you would have asked the Bishops to consider it, and to forward your views. Thus would you have commended to all, not only your motive and intention, but also your actions, by your showing proper deference to those whom you promised to obey; and in so doing you would have won thousands of earnest and sensible men whom you have estranged. Whereas the arrogant, insidious way in which you have tried to bring in your innovations has stamped your movement as Romish; and your open defiance of all episcopal authority makes you, of course, appear in the light of schismatics.

Thus, while the men of another generation, of whom only one is yet living, did stir up our very hearts, even though we did not always agree with them, do you convince neither judgment nor heart, but only raise a smile and suspicion. And while doing the work of your foes, you also do your best to rend asunder into yet greater divisions the Church of England, which will soon exist only in name and in the tears and regrets of her sons; unless her loyal Clergy and laity be up and doing, and her Bishops exert themselves to defend her existence and to secure her rights.

The above was already in print, when the Resolutions of the Upper House of Convocation on Ritualism were made public. The general satisfaction they gave to all honest and loyal Churchmen, is great indeed. But greater will it yet be if the Bishops having thus spoken out with one consent and one mouth, really set to work to promote greater order and uniformity in the services of the Church, and thus, also, let us hope, greater union and unanimity among the Clergy than there is at present.

If they be in earnest, there is for them work enough ready to hand. Not, indeed, that of straining at a few unoffending gnats, but of dealing with camels that do not mind Bishops. The present opportunity, therefore, would seem a fitting one for the prelates of the realm to agree on some definite outline or form of ritual and ceremonial in public worship, distinctly and honestly Anglican, and such as to satisfy, on the one hand, the reasonable demands of Churchmen for what is reverent and decorous, and on the other hand also, such as to raise no insuperable difficulty in the way of those who, having left the Church, and being accustomed to a simpler form of worship, may wish to return to her fold.

THE END.

WILLIAM STEVENS, PRINTER, 37, BELL YARD, TEMPLE BAR.

THE REV. S. C. MALAN.

In the Press, in One Vol., Crown 8vo,

SERMONS

BY

GABRIEL, BISHOP OF IMERETH.

ON

Faith, Eternal Punishments, and Other Subjects.

Translated from the Georgian

BY THE REV. S. C. MALAN, M.A.,
VICAR OF BROADWINDSOR.

LONDON:
SAUNDERS, OTLEY, AND CO.,
66, BROOK STREET, W.

THE REV. S. C. MALAN.

In the Press, in One Vol., 8vo,

AN OUTLINE

OF

THE EARLY JEWISH CHURCH;

FROM A CHRISTIAN POINT OF VIEW.

IN TWO BOOKS.

BOOK I. THE PATRIARCHS.   BOOK II. THE CHURCH IN THE WILDERNESS.

BY THE REV. S. C. MALAN, M.A.,
VICAR OF BROADWINDSOR.

LONDON:
SAUNDERS, OTLEY, AND CO.,
66, BROOK STREET, W.

66, *Brook Street, London, W.*

1867.

Messrs. Saunders, Otley, & Co.'s

LIST OF NEW BOOKS AND NEW EDITIONS.

Now ready, in one volume, demy 8vo, with Portrait and Illustrations.
PRICE ONE GUINEA.

The Forest and the Field,

By H. A. L., 'The Old Shekarry," Author of ' The Hunting Grounds of the Old World,' ' The Camp Fire.' &c.

Contents—Steeplechasing in the Deccan, Elephant, Tiger, Leopard, Panther and Bear Shooting—Hunting on High Altitudes—Ibex, Burrel, Thaar, Musk Deer, Snow Bear, Ovis-ammon, Wild Horse, and Bonchour stalking in the Himalaya -Reminiscences of the Danube and the Crimea—Sporting Trip to the West Coast of Africa, Gorilla, Chimpanzee, Hippopotamus and Wild Cattle Shooting—Pencillings in Austria during the late Campaign—Chamois Hunting in the Tyrol—Exploration Trips in different parts of the World, &c.

In 1 vol., with Illustrations, New Edition.

The Hunting Grounds of the Old World.

By H. A. L., " The Old Shekarry."

In 3 vols, post 8vo, £1 11s. 6d.

Personal Reminiscences of Eminent Men.
By CYRUS REDDING,
Author of 'Past Celebrities,' 'Fifty Years' Recollections, Literary and Personal,' 'Memoirs of Thomas Campbell,' &c. &c.

In 1 vol. 8vo. 21s.

Memoirs and Services of the late Lieut.-Gen. Sir S. B. Ellis, K.C.B., &c., Royal Marines.
From his own Memoranda. Edited by LADY ELLIS.

"The book has the rare merit of being short, and it is homely and unpretending like the author, who left behind him in its pages the best possible example of what an officer of marines should be."-*Saturday Review.*

In 2 vols. post 8vo, 21s.

The American Crisis;
Or, Pages from the Note Book of a State Agent during the Civil War.
By Colonel JOHN LEWIS PEYTON, L.B., F.R.G.S., &c.

Dedicated, by permission, to the Right Rev. the Lord Bishop of Oxford.—In 1 vol. Second and Cheaper Edition, post 8vo., wi Portraits, Maps, and Illustrations, price 9s. cloth.

The Universities Mission to East Central Africa.
From its Commencement to its Withdrawal from the Zambezi.
By the Rev. HENRY ROWLEY.
One of the Two Survivors of Bishop Mackenzie's Clerical Staff.

In 1 vol. crown 8vo,

The Church Sacraments and the Ministry.
By the Rev. W. R. CLARK, Vicar of Taunton.

In 1 vol. 8vo, cloth, 18s.

An Outline of the Jewish Church, from a Christian Point of View.
By the Rev. C. S. MALAN, M.A., Vicar of Broadwindsor.

In 1 vol., post 8vo., 6s., bevelled boards.
Scriptural Studies:
OUR CHURCH AND OUR TIMES.
BY THE AUTHOR OF "THOUGHTFUL MOMENTS," &c. &c.

In 1 vol. 8vo, 18s.
SECOND EDITION, with PREFACE by REV. R. F. LITTLEDALE, LL.D.
Essays on Liturgiology and Church History.
By the Rev. JOHN MASON NEALE, D.D., Warden of Sackville College.
With an Appendix on Liturgical Quotations from the Isapostolic Fathers, by the Rev. GERARD MOULTRIE, M.A.

NEW EDITION.
In 1 vol. crown 8vo, 3s. 6d.
Sermons on the Gospels,
From Easter to Trinity.
By A COUNTRY PARSON.

In 1 vol. 8vo, 12s.
London Pauperism amongst Jews and Christians.
By J. H. STALLARD, M.B., Lond.
Author of "The Female Casual," &c., &c.

In Crown 8vo., price 3s. 6d., cloth,
The Female Casual and Her Lodging.
With a complete Scheme for the Regulation of Workhouse Infirmaries.
By J. H. STALLARD, M.B., Lond.,
Author of "London Pauperism," "Workhouse Hospitals, &c.

In 1 vol. fcp. 4to, with Eight full-page Illustrations.
Stories from Early French History.
A Book for Children.
By AGNES LUSHINGTON.

Uniform with "The History of a Bit of Bread." In 2 vols. small 8vo, 9s.
The Little Kingdom, or the Servants of the Stomach.
A New Series of Letters to the Young upon the Life of Man and of Animals.
By JEAN MACE.
Translated from the French.

In 1 vol. post 8vo.
Words in Season.
A Book for Girls. By SYDNEY COX.

In 2 vols, post 8vo, £1 1s.
The Modern Pedagogue.
By J. RHYS.

In 3 vols. post 8vo.
The Romance of Cleaveside.
A NOVEL.
By the Author of "Ruth Baynard's Story," "Mary Eaglestone's Lover," &c.

In 3 vols. post 8vo.
Raymond:
An Exceptional Biography.
By HARRY MORELAND.

In 3 vols. post 8vo.
Mr. Frayne's Patient.
A Novel. By M. GREER.

In 1 vol. post 8vo.
Reginald Vane.
A Story of Military Life.
By E. TUDOR RISK, R.M., Lt. Inf.

In 1 vol. post 8vo.
Capital Punishment.
A TALE.
By Mrs. HODGSON,

In 3 vols. post 8vo.
A Wife and Not a Wife.
A NOVEL.
By CYRUS REDDING.

In 3 vols. post 8vo.
Mynchin.
A Novel. By an Unknown Author.

In 3 vols. post 8vo.
The Gowers of Glenarne.
A NOVEL.
By D. R. JONES.

In 3 vols.
The Fortune of Fairstone.
A NOVEL.
By R. WHIELDON BADDELEY,
Author of "Two to One on the Major," &c.

In 2 vols. post 8vo.
The Heir of Maberly.
A NOVEL.
By H. G. STURKEY, M.D.

In 3 vols., post 8vo.
Adventures of an Arcot Rupee.
By Major Charles F. Kirby, Retired List Madras Army.

In 3 vols. post 8vo.

The House of Rochfort.
A NOVEL.
By W. PLATT, author of "Angelo Lyons," "Betty Westminster."

In 3 vols. post 8vo.,

Briars and Thorns.
A NOVEL.
By BLANCHE MARRYATT.

"We can conscientiously congratulate Miss Marryatt on having written this story, and predict for her great future success."—*Observer*.

"Miss Blanche Marryatt possesses the rarest gift in woman — that of viewing things through the medium of her intellect and reason, and not through the mists of feminine feelings and passions."—*Press and St. James's Chronicle*.

"This lady is endowed with considerable creative talent."—*Bell's Messenger*.

"A most entertaining novel."—*London Review*.

"The tale is both spiritedly written. and interesting."—*Dispatch*.

In 3 vols. post 8vo.

The Wife's Peril.
A ROMANCE.
By J. I. LOCKHART.

In 3 vols. post 8vo.

Idols of Clay.
A NOVEL.
By Mrs. GORDON SMYTHIES, Author of "The Jilt," "True to the Last," &c.

"It will find numerous admirers."—*Observer*.

"A book that will arrest and rivet the attention."—*Press and St. James's Chronicle*.

"Mrs. Gordon Smythies has indeed given us sensational fare."—*John Bull*.

"Mrs. Gordon Smythies has been very felicitous in the choice of a subject for her new novel."—*Sun*.

"Lovers of mysterious and exciting incident will doubtless bestow on the tale warm approval."—*Dispatch*.

"Mrs. Gordon Smythies has given us a rich feast of startling sensations."—*London Review*.

"There are thousands who will read 'Idols of Clay' with intense interest." *Weekly Times*.

NEW EDITION, 1 vol., 4to, *with Eight full-page Engravings*.

Barefooted Birdie.
A SIMPLE TALE.
By T. O'T.
Edited by CHARLES FELIX, Author of "Velvet Lawn," &c.

In post 4to, 7s. 6d., with numerous Illustrations by E. Froment.
The Princess Ilsee.
A Fairy Legend.

In 1 vol. post 4to, with Eight full-page Engravings, by A. WIEGAND.
The History of Prince Perrypets.
A FAIRY TALE.
By L. KNATCHBULL HUGESSEN.

In 1 vol. fcp. 8vo.
Great Grandmama's Workbox.
A BOOK OF FAIRY TALES.
By Mrs. LUSHINGTON.

In 2 vols, post 8vo.
The Young Earl.
A STORY.
By S. S. HAWTREY.

In 1 vol. post 8vo., 10s. 6d., bevelled boards.
Meta's Letters.
A TALE.
By Mrs. ENSELL,
Author of "The Pastor's Family."

Post 4to., 7s. 6d., with Nine Page Illustrations.
The Maiden of the Iceberg.
A TALE, IN VERSE.
By SELINA GAYE,
Author of "Ivon," &c.

In 1 vol., fcap. 8vo, 2s. 6d.
The Last Crusader:
A POEM.
In Four Cantos.

HISTORY, BIOGRAPHY, ETC.

THE "ALABAMA."

Now ready, in 2 vols. post 8vo, Second Edition, 24s.

The Cruise of the "Alabama" and the "Sumter."

From the PRIVATE JOURNALS, &c., of CAPTAIN SEMMES, C.S.N., AND OTHER OFFICERS.

With ILLUSTRATIONS, CORRESPONDENCE, &c.

Second Edition.

"They are useful less for the novelty of the information which they convey than for authenticating, summarizing, and methodizing numerous little histories that have long since been notorious."—*Times*.

"The conduct and courage of Captain Semmes in action were worthy of his cause and of his reputation, but the qualities by which he will be hereafter memorable will rather be the judgment with which he executed his plans. Whether that peace for which Captain Semmes sighed during the lonely hours of his cruise comes soon or late, this at least is certain, that the flag under which the 'Alabama' cruised has contributed a memorable episode to the naval history of the world."—*Saturday Review*.

"A simple, straightforward, and most interesting narrative of a successful enterprise, which must always hold a prominent place in the annals of naval warfare."—*Press*.

"Captain Semmes' Journals will do much not only to keep alive the fame of the Alabama in our national records, but to enable English men to appreciate the character of her daring commander as a true gentleman and patriot, as well as a skilful and dashing sailor. The tale of the gallant "Alabama" will not easily be forgotten in the memory of Englishmen."—*John Bull*.

"We regard the volumes before us, authentic as they may be deemed in the source, as a very useful record of a very memorable episode in naval warfare."—*Globe*.

"An authentic account of the career of Captain Semmes—at least so far as it has been connected with the 'Alabama' and 'Sumter,'—compiled from his private journals and other papers, cannot fail to be read with interest both by friend and foe."—*Dispatch*.

"The name of Captain Semmes has gone forth into all lands wherever printed news can penetrate or the trumpet-tongue of fame is heard. Henceforth the name of Semmes is historic, and "290" is a charmed number."—*Illustrated London News*.

In 1 vol. post 8vo, with Portrait of the Alabama, 6s.

The Log of the Alabama and the Sumter:

Abridged from the Library Edition of "THE CRUISE OF THE ALABAMA."

"This volume will be read with great interest. Written in a frank, manly, unaffected style."—*London Review*.

"The Alabama's raid upon the ocean is presented in a moderate sized volume, which will be a favourite one in the library of a man of war."—*Churchman*.

"In absorbing interest this volume is not surpassed by any contemporaneous publication."—*Sunday Times*.

"We welcome this remarkable narrative in its present handsome and convenient form. It is abridged from the library edition, but nothing essential is omitted, and the circle of its possessors will now be greatly extended."—*Dispatch*.

Also a Cheap Edition in boards, 2s

In 1 vol. post 8vo, s. 6d ·

The War in America. 1863—64.
By EDWARD POLLARD,
Late Editor of the "Richmond Examiner," now a Prisoner.

"The author has given us the only connected account which we possess of a campaign remarkable for the numbers of those who have perished in its battles."—*Churchman*.

"The details of the great conflict are very instructive."—*Observer*.

"The volume contains the best connected account yet published of the Western campaigns from the invasion of Maryland and the battle of Gettysburg, down to the last actions before Petersburg, and of Grant's, Sherman's, and Bank's campaigns in the West and South West."—*Reader*.

"Those who wish to have a bird's-eye view of the past year's campaigns cannot do better than peruse this volume."—*Dispatch*.

"Mr. Pollard's volume takes a wide scope. He writes, indeed chiefly of the war, but he writes as a civilian, and deals with many political matters which had an undoubted if an indirect effect on the campaigns. With all these subjects and very much more, Mr. Pollard's book ably deals with."—*Standard*.

"Of Mr. Pollard's style it may be said that it is tolerably clear. As a summary of events, however, this volume may be found not entirely useless or unacceptable."—*Daily News*.

COMPLETION OF MR. ARNOLD'S DALHOUSIE ADMINISTRATION.

In 2 vols. 8vo, 15s. each.

The Marquis of Dalhousie's Administration of British India.

By EDWIN ARNOLD, M.A., University College, Oxford.
Late Principal, Poonah College; and Fellow of the University of Bombay.

Contents of Vol. I.
The Acquisition and Administration of the Punjaub.

Contents of Vol. II.
The Annexation of Pegu, Nagpore, and Oude, and a General Review of Lord Dalhousie's Rule in India.

"To those who look with interest on Indian affairs this work will doubtless afford considerable gratification. Undoubtedly the period of Lord Dalhousie's administration in India was a brilliant one."—*Morning Advertiser*.

"Of the work as a whole it would be impossible to express any judgment which was not highly favourable. It is full of information; it is almost everywhere guided by the calm and impartial spirit of a true historian; its style is always vigorous and sometimes brilliant. It is indeed a timely and a valuable contribution to the History of British India."—*Morning Star*.

"Mr. Arnold does ample justice to the grasp of Lord Dalhousie's mind, the dignity of his character, and the generosity of his heart; and the 'History' which tells this strange conversion of scattered barbarous, corrupt, and oppressed heathen principalities into a British Empire, stands forth with all the splendid vividness of an historical epic."—*Daily Telegraph*.

"Mr. Arnold's work, however, while its animated style carries the reader on, is a valuable contribution to the history of the period with which it is concerned, and his judgment of Lord Dalhousie's character, as well as his public policy, seems to have been formed with impartiality."—*Guardian*.

Dedicated, by permission, to the Right Rev. the Lord Bishop of Oxford.—In 1 vol. Second and Cheaper Edition, post 8vo., with Portraits, Maps, and Illustrations, price 9s., cloth.

The Universities Mission to East Central Africa,
From its Commencement to its Withdrawal from the Zambezi.
By the Rev. HENRY ROWLEY,
One of the Two Survivors of Bishop Matkenzie's Clerical Staff.

"His (Mr. Rowley's) purpose is apparently to vindicate the judgment of those by whom it (the Mission) was undertaken, and to preserve a fair record of the efforts which failed to obtain a successful result. Probably he will not materially alter the general opinion as to the wisdom of the attempt. He has indeed illustrated, by a candid narrative the genuine heroism of Bishop Mackenzie and his followers; and if heroism were the one thing desirable in missionaries, there would be little cause for complaint. As it is, we are rather reminded of the criticism, 'It is magnificent, but it is not war.' The missionaries seem to have hurled themselves as thoughtlessly against the heathenism of Africa as the Light Brigade went in against the Russian Artillery at Balaclava."—*Saturday Review.*

"All our readers who have taken any interest—and which of them has not?—in the Central African Mission, or in the noble life and heroic death of Bishop Mackenzie, should make a point of reading this book. It will probably modify in many respects the opinions they may have formed about that grand but calamitous enterprise from the imperfect and fragmentary information which is all that has been hitherto in their hands. Mr. Rowley is an excellent writer, simple, and direct, he tells us exactly what we want to know, in language which nobody can mistake, while his descriptions of natives and scenery show that he is a man of acute and accurate observation, with a strong feeling for the picturesque, and an unusual power of communicating his impressions."—*Guardian.*

"Those who look with the greatest coldness on missionary efforts can scarcely deny—if they will take the pains to read this book—that Bishop Mackenzie and his noble army of martyrs did good service in Central Africa. As a piece of literary work Mr. Rowley's book is well done; it is free from the unskilful arrangement and wearisome iteration which have marred the value of several books of African trrvel, The style is manly, clear, and unaffected; the author is modest and reticent about his own achievements, and writes with uniform good temper and forbearance. The woodcuts, chiefly from Mr. Rowley's own sketches, form an attractive adjunct to the text."—*Times.*

"Mr. Rowley's volume is an excellent account of a corner of the world absolutely unknown except from Dr. Livingstone having passed through it."—*Westminster Review.*

"The volume is a readable and interesting one. Mr. Rowley has told the whole story well, showing judgment, taste, snd feeling. His book is much superior to the ordinary Mission books."—*Athenæum.*

"To those who delight to hear of cheerful endurance of hardship—real hardship, famine, war, and pestilence —of honest endeavours to raise the savage out of his degraded condition —of steadfast faith rising over every obstacle,—this book will be deeply interesting."—*Cuhrch Times.*

"Mr. Rowley has done excellent service in writing this book. In tone and spirit it rises superior to anything of the sort with which we are acquainted; and we shall be very much mistaken if the nonsense that has found favour on the subject of the African race through the representations of mere travellers and men of the world, and the crude theories of anthropologists and so-called "men of science," does not receive its quietus from the circulation of this intelligent and undoubtedly truthful missionary book."—*Churchman.*

"Written in a plain, scholar-like style, and bears the stamp of high principle and intelligence. A book so written could not fail to be interesting, and it is interesting."—*Church Review.*

"It is impossible to peruse this work without the deepest admiration for the noble men who composed it (the Mission); their constancy, their hopefulness, their unwearied labour, and the cheerfulness with which they bore the terrible trials to which they were exposed, are beyond all praise."—*Standard.*

"It is impossible to read this book without a feeling of pride at belonging to the nation which sent forth such brave and generous men, and of regret that such valuable lives should have been lost in so hopeless a cause. And yet, as Mr. Rowley well says, their lives have not been squandered in vain. The book which he has written is peculiarly valuable at the present moment, when there is a disposition in high places to maintain that black is the colour of the devil, and that every thing black is evil. That Africa abounds in wild beasts we know—most savage countries do—but that its inhabitants are not all wild beasts, as some travellers would have us believe, is more than proved by the interesting story of the Universities Mission to Central Africa."—*Pall Mall Gazette.*

"In spite of the sad details with which it abounds, the general impression which Mr. Rowley's book leaves upon the mind, is that mission work amongst the African races is as hopeful as amongst the heathen of any other country."—*Mission Life.*

"Mr. Rowley's work is chiefly a stirring account of travel and camp life, but it has the additional harm which the high motives of those engaged in it naturally affords. The many disasters, the famine, the sickness, the frequent deaths which befel them all are touchingly described; while the patience and courage of the whole company are sufficiently evident; the good and even beautiful qualities which appear in many of the natives receive full justice."—*Mission Field.*

"Besides the interest which must attach to the plain narrative by an eye-witness, of facts which we have so often discussed, the volume is in itself one of no ordinary merit. It is by far the most interesting and readable book of missionary tarvels which has for a long time past met our eye. The genial sympathy of the writer with all nature, and more especially with human nature—the judicious omission of the mere details of every day routine, which makes most books of travel so wearisome — and the breadth of view and gentle spirit which pervade every page—all contribute to this end; and it is altogether so graphic, unpretending, and natural, that at its close we can scarce tell whether the skill of the writer, or the tragic interest which belongs to its subject, lends it the greater charm."—*Ecclesiastic.*

In 1 vol. post 8vo, 3s. 6d.

The Right Hon. W. E. Gladstone, M.P.,
&c., &c.,
A POLITICAL REVIEW.
By R. MASHEDER, B.A., Author of "Dissent and Democracy."

In 2 vols. post 8vo, 21s.

The Soldier of Three Queens.
A Narrative of Personal Adventure.
By CAPTAIN HENDERSON.

In 1 vol. 8vo. 18s.

The History of the Cotton Famine,
FROM THE FALL OF SUMTER TO THE PASSING OF THE PUBLIC WORKS ACT.
By R. ARTHUR ARNOLD.

"Mr. Arnold's 600 pages are filled with facts and figures arranged in a lucid popular style, and from the great and permanent importance of the subject will be read with interest."—*Times.*

"The story of the cotton famine, as told by Mr. Arnold, has all the interest of a romance; the statistics, the figures, the reports of Mr. Farnall, the weekly returns of the Board of Guardians, are all so many threads of interest in the story. The book is well put together, carefully, and with a fairness and candour which entitle the author to high praise."—*Athenæum.*

"It traces in a clear and succinct manner the steps which were taken to meet a national calamity, as soon as the prospects of the cotton supply became darkened."—*Observer.*

"Mr. Arnold has put together all the facts with lucid minuteness, and enabled his readers to recall all the details of a struggle which reflected honour on British administration."—*Spectator.*

"We acknowledge the substantial merits of Mr. Arnold's work. He discusses with fairness, with temper, and we think with substantial justice, the various question which arose and became matter of controversy during the famine."—*London Review.*

"We congratulate Mr. Arnold on his having added a very valuable contribution to contemporary history. He has evidently bestowed very considerable pains in the collection of his facts, and arranged them in lucid order. His narrative has the merit of fidelity and of being free from partiality. It is complete in statement, and will always remain a standard book of reference with regard to the highly interesting events which it records."—*Herald.*

Also a New and Cheaper Edition, 1 *vol. post 8vo.,* 5s. 6d.

"Contains much valuable information."—*Star.*

"A valuable and comprehensive work."—*Dispatch.*

"These authentic records are most interesting, exhibiting as they do the unparalled success which attended the proceedings adopted to meet what at one time threatened to become an overwhelming calamity."—*Observer.*

In 1 vol. post 8vo, Second Edition, 6s.

The Danes in Camp:
LETTERS FROM SÖNDERBORG.
By the Honourable AUBERON HERBERT.

"This is a pleasantly written book, because it is exactly what it professes to be. Mr. Herbert's book is satisfactory to read, because it presents so strange a contrast to the average of the literary class to which he belongs. Its merit is that it is written because its author wishes to tell what he has seen and felt, and not because he wishes to produce an article that will sell. There are many lively and striking passages."—*Saturday Review.*

"The letters are well and gracefully written; they teem with interesting incidents and narrations; there is about them an air of probity, which instantly impresses the reader with the conviction that they contain only the truth; and all this is mingled with a good humour and moderation that win our confidence and deserve our respect."—*Daily News.*

"Mr. Herbert is an agreeable, manly writer, and English readers will respond gratefully to the generous sympathy and admiration which he expresses for the inhabitants of the little kingdom."—*Athenæum.*

"These interesting letters are dedicated to the writer's mother, the Countess Dowager of Carnarvon. They place the events of the siege graphically before the reader, in simple but forcible language. All that Mr. Herbert says claims our most careful attention."—*Reader.*

Cheap Edition, in 1 vol. post 8vo, 1s. 6d.

The Davenport Brothers:

A BIOGRAPHY OF IRA ERASTUS DAVENPORT AND WILLIAM HENRY DAVENPORT, commonly known as the "BROTHERS DAVENPORT."

With an Account of Eleven Years of Preternatural Phenomena and Extraordinary Physical and Psychical Manifestations.

By T. L. NICHOLS, M.D.,

Author of "Forty Years in America," &c.

"The book is replete with adventures calculated, we have no doubt, to produce in England effects similar to those experienced in America."—*Observer.*

"We commend this volume to our readers. Dr. Nichols had a difficult task, but it could not have been performed better."—*Herald.*

"The book which Dr. Nichols has published is precisely what is wanted. Short, simple, and clear; not pretending to explain, hardly, indeed, discussing the question as to whether explanation is possible; as fair a narrative written by a believer could possibly be—this volume commends itself to all. None can possibly find it dull."—*Standard.*

In 1 large vol. 8vo, the Second Edition, price 21s.

Australian Explorations.

JOHN McDOUALL STUART'S JOURNALS OF EXPLORATIONS IN AUSTRALIA from 1858 to 1862.

Edited by WILLIAM HARDMAN, M.A., F.R.G.S., &c.

Illustrated with a Portrait of the author, and 12 page Engravings on Wood, drawn by George French Angas, from Sketches taken during the Expedition, and accompanied by a carefully-prepared Map of the Explorer's Route across the entire Continent.

"A very large and valuable addition to our geographical knowledge of Australia."—*Observer.*

"Worthy of being ranked amongst the most important in the History of Australian discovery."—*Morning Advertiser.*

"To dilate on the value of the work to the very large number who are directly or indirectly interested in Australian progress is superfluous."—*Dispatch.*

"It is impossible to refrain from the strongest admiration of the narrative, given in his own Journal, in which so much unpretending unconscious heroism is evinced, such simple devotion to the *end* of his enterprise; thankfulness, not self-laudation at its accomplishment, hold ing his life so lightly so that his *duty* might be done."—*Globe.*

"These journals abound in interesting information, and have a special charm as living records of what the discoverer has seen and done."—*Examiner.*

"We can commend the book to the careful perusal of those who wish to appreciate something of the future of Australia."—*Morning Star.*

"The conductor of the expedition has earned lasting fame for the sterling qualities which he proved himself to possess. Throughout the toilsome journeys, of which he has given a minute and graphic account, he evinced every qualification which should characterise the leader of such expeditions."—*Morning Post.*

In 2 vols. post 8vo. with an Introduction and Appendices, 21s.

Secret History of a Polish Insurrection.
By H. SUTHERLAND EDWARDS,
Late Special Correspondent of the *Times* in Poland.

In 2 vols. post 8vo, with Portrait, 21s.

Belle Boyd in Camp and Prison.
Written by HERSELF.
With an INTRODUCTION by a FRIEND OF THE SOUTH.

"Her memoirs are very ably and graphically written. They are useful so far as they exemplify the difference between American and English society."—*Morning Post.*

"'Belle Boyd in Camp and Prison' is one of those books into which the whole soul and spirit of the writer has evidently passed—which are too earnest for artistic construction, too real and heartfelt either for self concealment or self display."—*Saturday Review.*

"To say that these volumes are interesting would be far short of the truth. They are perfectly thrilling, and we strongly recommend all our readers whichever side they take of the controversy, to get them and judge for themselves."—*John Bull.*

"Linked for ever with the story of that fatal American war is the name of Belle Boyd, and this book, written by herself, possesses such deep interest of wonder and truth, that it cannot fail of general acceptance and popularity. Belle Boyd in Camp and Prison is *the* book of the season."—*Court Circular.*

"Belle Boyd's book will be read with interest, and will no doubt make a great sensation."—*Observer.*

"The contents of these volumes are extremely interesting."—*Reader.*

"It is pleasantly and on the whole modestly written."—*Index.*

"Belle Boyd's adventures surpass the best contrived fictions of our most popular writers."—*Morning Advertiser.*

"Will be read with avidity."—*Sunday Times.*

"Full of vivid glimpses of the late war."—*Globe.*

"In these volumes we have from her own pen the story of her daring deeds, her hairbreadth escapes and her unmerited sufferings. A narrative of extreme interest, all the more attractive because natural and unaffected."—*London Review.*

"The book is one which is certain to obtain popularity, and to be speedily in the hands of most readers.'—*Churchman.*

"Possesses high claims to attention."—*Literary Gazette.*

"The book is undoubtedly a remarkable one."—*Dispatch.*

"Miss Belle Boyd (now Mrs. Hardinge) may fairly claim a niche beside those earlier heroines; having in one respect even a better right to the name of warrior than any of them, since she actually received a regular commission as Captain in the Confederate Army, and was attached to Stonewall Jackson's staff as one of his aides-de-camp."—*Evening Standard.*

"The story of the adventures, misfortunes, imprisonments, and persecutions of Mrs. Hardinge, better known as Belle Boyd, will do much to relieve the Federals of the stigma under which they have been labouring of treating their prisoners with harshness and brutality."—*Post.*

"Belle Boyd may well be contented with the recollection that in the fearful struggle which is now terminated she played no inglorious part."—*Morning Herald.*

"Doubly attractive, not only as telling a tale of deeds of daring skilfully executed, and dangers and hardships courageously confronted and endured, far surpassing in interest the wildest imagination of the sensation novelist."—*Standard.*

"Modestly and simply written and we think our readers will rise from the perusal with a true sympathy for its fair writer."—*Guardian.*

"The name of Belle Boyd is well known to all who took an interest in the late civil war in America."—*London Review.*

"There are few persons conversant with the American correspondence of our leading Journals during the late awful struggle of the South against the North, to whom the name of Belle Boyd, the Rebel Spy, is not known."—*Young Englishwoman.*

THEOLOGY.

Vol. III. 8vo, completing the work, 21s.

The History of the Church of England,

From the DEATH OF ELIZABETH to the PRESENT TIME
By the Rev. GEORGE G. PERRY, M.A.
Rector of Waddington, late Fellow and Tutor of Lincoln College. Oxford.

"Written in an easy style, and in a moderate, sensible spirit. Mr. Perry is, apparently, a good Churchman, belonging to no party, and desirous of doing justice to Nonconformists as well as to opposing schools in the Church."—*Reader.*

"A most useful and ably written work. The spirit in which the whole question of Church history is treated is highly creditable to the author, and throughout exhibits liberal, enlightened, and tolerant views."—*Observer.*

"The whole makes a pleasant and readable history of the period chronicled. Mr. Perry manifests a desire to maintain the sound doctrine and discipline of the Church."—*English Churchman.*

"Our author never shirks any portion of work which fairly belongs to him; and above all, he has no bias but for the broad plain truth. Mr. Perry's work must take its place as the companion of Southey and Short, not only in the Library of every theological student, but every reader of history."—*Herald.*

"This valuable and important work is now complete, and Mr. Perry has the honour of filling up what has long been wanting in our ecclesiastical literature."—*Clerical Journal.*

THE REV. S. C. MALAN.

In 1 vol. Crown 8vo. 4s. cloth.

Ritualism.

By the Rev. S. C. MALAN, M.A., of Balliol College, Oxford, and Vicar of Broadwindsor.

In 1 vol. Crown 8vo., 5s.

Sermons,

By GABRIEL, Bishop of IMERETH.

On Faith, Eternal Punishment, and other Subjects. To which are added, by the same Author, an Exposition of the Lord's Prayer, and of the Beautitudes. Translated and Edited from the Georgian, by the Rev. S. C. MALAN, M.A., Vicar of Broadwindsor.

In 1 vol. crown 8vo. 6s.

A History of the Georgian Church.

Translated from the Russian of P. IOSELIAN, by the Rev. S. C. MALAN, M.A., Vicar of Broadwindsor.

In 1 vol. post 8vo, bevelled edges, 9s., cloth.

Thoughtful Moments.
By ONE OF THE PEOPLE.

"A thoughtful book, highly suggestive of important matter to both clergy and laity."—*Clerical Journal.*

"The author has the merit of stating his views with clearness and ability."—*Star.*

Price 8d. and 1s.

Parish Hymn Book.
Edited by the Rev. H. W. Beadon, the Rev. Greville Phillimore, and the Rev. James Russell Woodford.

---

1 vol. small 8vo, antique, 7s. 6d.

Sermons,
By the late Rev. C. T. ERSKINE, M.A.
Incumbent of St. Michael's, Wakefield. With a Memoir of his Life, and a preface by the Bishop of Brechin.

"The Sermons are far above the average of such compositions, and in many parts they are remarkable for the originality of thought which they possess. A devout and reverent spirit, moreover, pervades every sermon."—*Observer.*

"Mr. Erskine's Sermons are thirty-one in number, and they are all interesting."—*Clerical Journal.*

"A work of absorbing interest, and one which none can well read without feeling infinitely the better for it. The volume is got up with singular neatness."—*Church Review.*

"Mr. Erskine's style is vigorous and thoughtful."—*Literary Churchman.*

"These Sermons will be treasured by many, and pondered over by many, who knew the sterling excellence of him by whom they were written and preached. The memoir of his life has evidently been a labour of love, and affectionately depicts a character which no one can study without deriving benefit from it."—*Scottish Guardian.*

"The fervour, simplicity, and faith evinced in these discourses are worthy of the best age."—*Globe.*

"Of Mr. Erskine's Sermons we can hardly speak in too high terms. Calm, thoughtful, mild, and yet austere, they are instinct with Catholic truth and Catholic faith."—*Churchman.*

In 1 vol. 8vo, post 8vo, 6s. 6d.

Modern Scepticism in relation to Modern Science;
IN REFERENCE TO THE DOCTRINES OF COLENSO, HUXLEY, LYELL, DARWIN, &c.
By J. R. YOUNG, Author of "Science Elucidative of Scripture," &c.

"Mr. Young brings to the discussion of his subject a clear and elegant style—no small advantage to the reader, when the subject itself is recondite or little known. The author argues like a philosopher and writes like a gentleman."—*Literary Gazette.*

"The book is well worthy the perusal of those interested in the discussion of these questions."—*Press.*

"The work is an admirable antidote to the scepticism of the age."—*Homilist.*

"Those who are pained at the assumed antagonism between Science and Revelation, will read Mr. Young's volume with sincere pleasure, and will thank him for having taken up the cause of truth so successfully."—*Public Opinion.*

"The author writes in a correct and pleasing style, eschewing, as far as it is possible, anything that might approach to scientific pedantry of language."—*London Review.*

MISCELLANEOUS.

In 8vo. price 10s. 6d., Second Edition.
The Cotton Trade:
Its Bearing upon the Prosperity of Great Britain and Commerce of the American Republics considered in Connection with the System of Negro Slavery in the Confederate States.

By GEORGE McHENRY.

"Contains a mass of information on most matters at all involved in the origin of the disruption among the whilom United States."—*Glasgow Courier.*

---

1 vol. post 8vo, illustrated, 12s.
Hunting Tours,
By "CECIL."

"The book is a contribution to the subject which has long been wanted, and which reflects the greatest credit upon the author for his composition, and the publishers for their discrimination in bringing it before the public in its present attractive form."—*Sporting Gazette.*

"'Hunting Tours' will afford interest and amusement to all classes of readers. The work is admirably illustrated by E. Corbet, and beautifully got up both as to type and binding."—*Sporting Review.*

"There is scarcely any topic connected with the hunting field which is not treated with fulness and force, in 'Cecil's' picturesque and animated sketches."—*Morning Post.*

"'Cecil' has performed the task he undertook with ability and zeal, and his 'Hunting Tours' should be found on the library table of every sporting man."—*Sun.*

"A volume which cannot fail to prove of much interest to sportsmen, and we commend it to their especial attention."—*Oxford Journal.*

"Contains an immense amount of valuable information, such as only a veteran fox hunter of the first order could supply. 'Cecil's' pseudonym suffices to guarantee the excellence of his book."—*Press.*

"Written with a masterly knowledge of its subject * * * 'Cecil' writes like a gentleman: there is much that is very exciting and interesting in his book."—*Daily News.*

"Gives particulars respecting the various packs with which the author has hunted, narrates the fortunes of their several masters or whips, and chronicles here and there the particulars of a remarkably successful run."—*Sunday Times.*

In 1 vol. 8vo, half bound, £2 5s.
The Kennel Stud Book,
Containing Lists of the most celebrated Packs of Foxhounds; with the Pedigrees of Stud Hounds.

By CORNELIUS TONGUE ("Cecil"), Author of "Hunting Tours," &c.

In 8vo, cloth, 3s. 6d.
Shakspere Weighed in an Even Balance.
By the Rev. ALFRED POWNALL, M.A.,
Vicar of Trowse Newton and Fakenham, late Crosse's Theological Scholar, Cambridge, &c.

In Foolscap 8vo, cloth, Second Edition, 5s.

The History of a Bit of Bread.

Being Letters to a Child, on the Life of Man and of Animals.
By Jean Macé.
Translated from the French and edited by Mrs. ALFRED GATTY.
Author of "Parables from Nature," &c.

PART I. MAN.

"Mrs. Gatty has here favoured the public with a volume weighty in its matter, fasciuating in its form, and in its moral and religious tone above all praise."—*London Review.*

"This work, especially intended for the use of the young, explains in a manner both intelligible and interesting, 'the history of life as sustained and supported in the human race.'"—*Dispatch.*

"Written in a reverent spirit deserving of commendation—a fact that the name of the translator alone would guarantee."—*John Bull.*

"To Mrs. Gatty great praise is due. * * * * * The translation seems excellent. A charming little book."—*Church Review.*

"Let us commend this pleasant little book to parents and guardians throughout the length and breadth of the British dominions, since it is one of the very best of its class that we have met with."—*Bell's Messenger.*

"It exhibits the honest pains, the desire to please, the unmistakeable labour, which characterise all Mrs. Gatty undertakes for the acceptance of the public."—*Press.*

"This little book has reached its eighth edition on the other side of the Channel, having been adopted by the University Commission of Paris among their prize books."—*Athenæum.*

"Written for children, grown up people will read it with profit and pleasure. Eight editions have made the French public familiar with the original, and Mrs. Gatty has conferred no slight boon on the English by a translation which faithfully preserves its best features."—*Spectator.*

Also,
In Foolscap 8vo, cloth, 4s. 6d.

PART II. ANIMALS.
Completing the Work.

"We had the pleasure of noticing the first part some months ago. We can only repeat our words of praise. The fact is we cannot praise it enough. Everything which can contribute to a most charming and instructive book is here to be found. Exquisite humour, a highly moral tone, most useful instruction—what more can be wanted to make up an acceptable book? The translator has done her work so felicitously that the book reads like an original production."—*Church Review.*

"A charming guide to many important scientific subjects, necessary to be known by all persons aspiring to be considered well-educated."—*Clerical Journal.*

"As in the first part of this work the translator and editress, Mrs. Gatty has now and then slightly altered the original, with a view to rendering the illustrations more intelligible and interesting to the mind of an English child. We reiterate the opinion we have already expressed with regard to the first part of the present work—that it is a valuable little treatise, containing much that is interesting and instructive not only to children but to adults."—*London Review.*

"Though especially meant for children, and adapted to their capacity, it may nevertheless be read by their elders with profit; and its compactness, lucidity of arrangement, and absence of confusing detail, combined with humorous illustration, makes it extremely readable."—*Dispatch.*

Second and revised edition, post 8vo, 10s. 6d.

The Gouty Philosopher;

Or, THE OPINIONS, WHIMS, AND ECCENTRICITIES
OF JOHN WAGSTAFFE, ESQ., OF WILBYE GRANGE.
By CHARLES MACKAY.

In 1 vol. post 8vo. 2s.

Conyers Lea,

Or SKETCHES OF CHARACTER, MILITARY, MAGISTERIAL, AND EPISCOPAL.

By CYRIL THORNTON, M.A.

Cheap Edition.

NOVELS.

In 3 vols. post 8vo.

Philo:

A ROMANCE OF LIFE IN THE FIRST CENTURY.

By JOHN HAMILTON, M.A., Cantab.

In 2 vols., post 8vo, 21s.

Hena: or Life in Tahiti.

A NOVEL.

By Mrs. ALFRED HORT.

A NEW NOVEL by the Author of "THE UTTERMOST FARTHING."

THIRD, or "ATHENÆUM" EDITION, with Preface and Correspondence.
In 3 vols. post 8vo.

VICTORY DEANE.

A NOVEL.

By CECIL GRIFFITH,

Author of "The Uttermost Farthing."

"A book of power and of promise, and its power is of a true kind."—*Standard.*

"It arrests and fascinates the attention of the reader."—*Herald.*

"Strongly reminds us of Charlotte Bronte's best works."—*Globe.*

"The charm lies in the treatment, in the perfectly natural characters of Brand and Margaret, in the pathetic humility and simple lovingness of Victory, and in the fresh and original manner of relation. It is in the character of Victory that we see the traces of French influence. There is a certain subtle tenderness of delineation, a certain careful and minute analysis, and a steadfast chronicling of spiritual progress infuitely more after the French school than the English, and the story gains in interest thereby."—*Saturday Review.*

In 1 vol. post 8vo, 10s. 6d., bevelled boards.

The Romance of Mary Constant.
Written by Herself.

"A thoroughly healthy book like this, equally pure in thought and diction, with ample interest, and with almost every character drawn with a firm and accurate hand, is a great boon."—*Church and State Review.*

"The story is well written from first to last."—*Reader.*

In 3 vols. post 8vo.

The Uttermost Farthing.
A NOVEL.
By CECIL GRIFFITH.

"The story is one of character, influenced by accident, and the psychology of the thing is detailed and curious, and has, no doubt, been studied from the life."—*Reader.*

"A terrible prose tragedy; but it presents remarkable materials for powerful writing, and the author has turned them to the best possible account."—*Court Circular.*

"A good and gracefully written novel; the plot being cleverly conceived and well sustained. The strong, passionate, sisterly love here pourtrayed for an erring and unfortunate brother is tenderly and faithfully rendered. The whole book abounds in passages at once grand, pathetic, and natural."—*John Bull.*

"A work of very unusual promise; indeed, of more than promise; for it is itself, if not the best, decidedly one of the best, novels of the day. The plot is good and well worked out, and the characters drawn with a firm and skilful hand."—*Church and State Review.*

"How this, and much more is told, only a perusal of the story which we have barely indicated, will show; the involutions and perplexities of feeling and action, and the revelation of the inner struggle going on behind, what strikes us as one of the most painful positions ever penned."—*Globe.*

"The author is certainly deserving of praise for the novelty of plot in this book."—*Observer.*

"The author of 'The Uttermost Farthing' has written a novel which will make its readers anxious for another production of the same pen."—*Star.*

"Alan Valery's indolent, passionate character is well drawn. May Valery is excellently conceived."—*Press.*

"Of 'The Uttermost Farthing' we may conscientiously say, that taking story, style, and the skilful manner in which the plot is worked out together, there are few existing novels in our language which may justly be accorded a higher rank."—*Sun.*

"The book contains some touches of real feeling."—*Guardian.*

"Told with considerable power. The story is an interesting one."—*Churchman.*

In 3 vols. post 8vo.

Angelo Lyons.
A NOVEL.
By WILLIAM PLATT,
Author of "Yorke House," &c.

In 3 vols. post 8vo.

Snooded Jessaline;
Or, The Honour of a House.
A NOVEL.
By MRS. T. K. HERVEY.

In 1 vol. post 8vo, 10s. 6d.

Donnington Hall.

A NOVEL.

By the Rev. F. TALBOT O'DONOGHUE,
Author of "St. Knighton's Keive," &c.

"This volume contains a very pleasing story, thoroughly natural in its style and admirably written. The characters are well defined, and present a very charming homely group to the reader's notice."—*Observer.*

"A highly entertaining work, and one in which the reader's interest will seldom if ever flag. The material itself of which the story is composed is not rich; but the embroidery with which it is overlaid is tasteful. Many of the characters are hit off with much skill and effect, and the picture of the little child wife is singularly pleasing."—*Sunday Times.*

"The construction of the tale is simple; but its pleasant, unaffected style of narration makes it extremely readable."—*Dispatch.*

"Mr. O'Donoghue has written a volume which will be read with pleasure, more for its sketches of every-day clerical life than for any interest that gathers round it as a novel."—*Public Opinion.*

"A quiet serious story. The tone of the book throughout is kindly and genial."—*London Review.*

"'Donnington Hall' is an amusing and clever book."—*Western Morning News.*

"The society and scenery of the places in which the story is laid are described with the correctness of an artist who draws from nature.'—*Shipping nd Mercantile Gazette.*

In 3 vols. post 8vo.

Velvet Lawn.

A NOVEL.

By CHARLES FELIX, Author of "The Notting Hill Mystery."

"Strong and pervading interest there unquestionably is in the story."—*Observer.*

"A straightforward and workmanlike story, fairly interesting throughout. Mr. Felix is evidently a man of ability."—*Reader.*

"Such as admire an elaborately contrived plot, detailed in a fluent and easy style, will derive much pleasure from the perusal of the tale."—*Dispatch.*

"In character as well as incident, 'Velvet Lawn' is singularly rich, and it will unquestionably be a very popular novel."—*Press.*

"The plot appears to us to be original, and is certainly remarkable for its ingenuity."—*Athenæum.*

"The plot of 'Velvet Lawn' is exceedingly well conceived, and the interest never flags."—*Index.*

"It will find many readers, having attractions for the more thoughtful as well as the mere devourers of sensationalism."—*Herald.*

"There is a story, and that story is well told, so that it will command many readers."—*Globe.*

"It rises far above the ordinary run of novels."—*Daily News.*

In 3 vols. post 8vo.

Rington Priory.

A NOVEL. By ETHEL HONE.

"The moral is unobjectionable."—*Athenæum.*

"A very excellent novel of its class. Written with a natural force which suggests very little effort, it is free from affectation or strained effects."—*Reader.*

"Reminds us of 'Emma'. and 'Sense and Sensibility,' 'Pride and Prejudice,' and the rest of that mildly brilliant constellation."—*Globe.*

"'Rington Priory' is an interesting story. with an air of truthfulness."—*Press.*

"The incidents, conversations, and plot are eminently natural and interesting: and the entire tone of the novel so perfectly healthy, that we consider it a positive relief from the morbid works with which the modern press so almost uniformly teems."—*Star.*

In 2 vols. post 8vo.
Mr. Christopher Katydid (of Casconia).
A TALE.
Edited by MARK HEYWOOD.

"There are marks of cleverness in this tale. The author gives evidence of ability."—*Athenæum*.

"The reader may derive much entertainment from a series of clever sketches relating to persons, customs, and scenery, partly American, partly English."—*Observer*.

"Quaint in construction and singular in manner, may be taken as a true definition of this American story; the plot is amusing."—*Bell's Messenger*.

"There are some pleasant descriptions of country scenery, and the story is very amusing."—*Star*.

"Reveals to us some new and curious habits of life."—*Daily News*.

"The work has merits, and is not undeserving of perusal. It is a thoroughly trans-Atlantic tale, and the heroes and heroines whom it describes are refreshingly different from those of our native romance." *London Review*.

---

1 vol. post 8vo.
Passages in the Life of an Old Maid.

"Certainly above the average"—*Morning Post*.

"Full of interest and detailed in a lively natural style."—*Sun*.

"The style of writing is easy, and often amusing."—*Illustrated News*.

In 3 vols. post 8vo.
Percy Talbot.
A NOVEL.
By GEORGE GRAHAM.
Author of "Carstone Rectory," &c.

"Mr. Graham's style is varied and sparkling yet always clear and perspicuous. His descriptions are easy and pleasing; his characters are well conceived, and all live and breathe. There is a great freshness pervades the entire work, and it possesses a literary merit which will stand a comparison with almost any work of the day. We unhesitatingly recommend the book to our readers, and shall be glad again to encounter its author in a field in which he has already acquitted himself so well, and in which we are prepared to anticipate for him further and more signal triumphs."—*Sunday Times*.

"We have here a powerfully written tale. There is no overcrowding of the canvass, the secondary figures come in as mere accessories to three principal actors in the terrible drama. The mixture of good and evil in 'Percy Talbot' is well chosen."—*John Bull*.

"'Percy Talbot' is a novel that will, we feel certain, find many warm admirers. Mr. Graham has unquestionable talents for making a successful novel-writer, and produces quite a dramatic effect in his descriptive passages. Some of his characters, too, are excellent, both as to the conception and carrying out, altogether it is a story that will carry away most readers by its somewhat impetuous style and interesting well-sustained plot."—*Observer*.

"Written with a considerable knowledge of character. The book has great and growing interest, and the attention of the reader is rivetted as he turns over the pages. The dialogue throughout the book is exceedingly well done, and it cannot be doubted that the novel will be a great favourite at all the libraries, and indeed wherever it is read."—*Morning Star*.

"The style is vigorous and well sustained throughout. The principles of this book are unexceptionable, and its literary execution very satisfactory."—*Athenæum*.

"Written in a pleasant style, and with the best intentions. The author never sins against the laws of good manners, and he is evidently well acquainted with the usages of society. He appears to be actuated by strong but kindly feelings, and the book bears the impress of genuine earnestness. It is one which may be safely recommended to families, and it is likely to become a favourite with an immense class."—*London Review*.

In 1 vol. post 8vo, 10s. 6d.

The Notting Hill Mystery.

Compiled by CHARLES FELIX,

Author of "Velvet Lawn," etc.

"Much ingenuity is displayed in framing such of the circumstances as may credibly be supposed to have actually existed."—*Reader.*

"The chain of evidence is traced throughout with great minuteness, and the whole narrative is well calculated to awaken and sustain the interest of the reader."—*Observer.*

"This book is a singular and not wholly unsuccessful attempt to enlist the attention of the reader by the simple yet subtle analysis of crime. In doing so Mr. Felix reminds us, not unfavourably, of some of the prose writings of Edgar Poe. It is a strange story strangely told."—*Churchman.*

"We have seldom read anything more ingenious than the manner in which the circumstantial detail of the crime or crimes supposed to form the Notting Hill Mystery are narrated. Few more thoroughly mysterious, remarkable, and, we may add, more tantalising works have ever issued from the press."—*Sunday Times.*

"Among narratives of the mysterious, but circumstantial order, this is entitled to high rank."—*Dispatch.*

"To all whom a chain of intricate and peculiar evidence will interest we recommend this book, which surpasses anything in the same style we have met since Edgar Poe presented the world with his tales of the imagination."—*Court Circular.*

"It is a good specimen of the sensational story, of which the entire interest consists, not in the characters—which are scarcely indicated—but in the strangeness of the incidents and the complication of the plot."—*Guardian.*

In 3 vols. post 8vo.

Aubrey Court,

A NOVEL.

By FRANK LYFIELD.

"There are the makings of a good story in 'Aubrey Court.'"—*John Bull.*

"Whoever wishes to pass an agreeable hour or two, under the influence of light reading, free from violent spasmodic situations, may gratify his taste very largely by taking up Mr. Lyfield's clever specimen of fiction. Not only will pleasant writing be met with, but a plot will be discovered which preserves its unities throughout and terminates, as it had proceeded, very naturally. We know not whether 'Aubrey Court' is a first specimen of authorship; but if it be so, it gives not a few indications of intelligence and cleverness which may speedily be turned to considerable advantage."—*Bell's Messenger.*

"Too much praise cannot be awarded to the author of 'Aubrey Court' for the excessive care and attention he has shown in working out his plot. The story never flags from beginning to end; and if this be the first novel from Mr. Lyfield's pen, the public may look forward to even a greater treat when next he comes before them."—*Morning Post.*

"We have read every page of it with pleasure. It is a healthy, pure, interesting novel, conveying pleasant scenes of life at home and abroad, in good, plain, idiomatic English; and to say thus much is to raise 'Aubrey Court' to a height immeasurably above that occupied by the large majority of English works of fiction."—*Sunday Times.*

"The moral tone of the book is unimpeachable. 'Aubrey Court' is of more than average merit."—*Churchman.*

"The characters are so skilfully drawn, and the style is at once so lively and so genial, that the tale cannot fail to be read with pleasure by such as possess healthy literary taste, and recognise the conscientiousness with which the author strives to copy nature."—*Dispatch.*

In 3 vols. post 8vo.

Macaria.
A NOVEL.
By AUGUSTA J. EVANS,
Author of "Beulah," &c.

"The tone is high, the language chaste and pure, the characters noble, and the purpose laudable."—*Bell's Messenger.*

"The work is written with much ability, and striking incidents follow each other in such rapid succession that the interest is sustained throughout."—*Morning Advertiser.*

"In many respects the book is pleasing and the style is often forcible, and the moral tone is unobjectionable."—*Observer*

"Written in an earnest and enthusiastic tone. As another evidence of the strong emotions which animate the hearts of the women of the South, and which of themselves are sufficient to proclaim the deathless endurance of the struggle for Southern independence, 'Macaria' has an interest peculiarly its own."—*Sun.*

"Much that is really noble and excellent. The picture drawn by Miss Evans of the heroic deeds, the self-abnegation, of man and woman in the struggle, cannot but excite our admiration, and there is much power of actual description, especially in her account of the little vessel which runs the blockade into Mobile."—*Globe.*

"The author's heart is evidently in her work, and many portions of it are marked by an eloquent earnestness which cannot fail to enlist the sympathy of her readers. No slight amount of artistic feeling also is displayed in it."—*Dispatch.*

"'Macaria' is a remarkable book, and one of undeniable power: full of the impulsive, fiery, demonstrative spirit of the Southern States. Passages of real pathos and sublimity abound in it. The book gives a vivid picture of the self-sacrifice and patriotic devotion which animate the Confederacy."—*Guardian.*

In 2 vols. post 8vo.

Uncle Angus.
A NOVEL.
By MARY S. G. NICHOLS.
Author of "Uncle John," "Agnes Morris," &c.

"Written in a kindly pleasant tone, the characters are natural and well drawn, and upon the whole there is much to praise and little to find fault with, and it is a book that may with confidence be placed in the hands of youthful readers."—*Observer.*

"A very pleasant, genial, and clever story. We must leave our readers to become acquainted with it themselves, quite sure that they will not repent the trouble."—*Dispatch.*

"Genial, clever, and interesting."—*Bell's Messenger;*

"The chief merit of this novel lies in the delicate perception of character displayed by the author, and in the skill with which the incidents of the story are made to develope the peculiarities of the actors. A book which is very charming indeed."—*Morning Post.*

"Glimpses of feeling and indications of character which show what the writer might do."—*Globe.*

"A decidedly amusing novel."—*Reader.*

"A readable and a pleasant book."—*Sunday Times.*

"'Uncle Angus' will be read with pleasure. Mrs. Nichols evidently knows what she is about in novel-writing, and very cleverly contrives to make a good story out of simple materials. There is a great deal of clever portraiture in the book."

"'Uncle Angus' has great interest, and will doubless be favourably thought of by all by whom it is read."—*Star.*

---

1 vol. post 8vo. 5s.

Why Paul Ferroll Killed his Wife.
By the Author of "PAUL FERROLL." Fourth Edition.

TALES, ETC.

Foolscap 8vo, with Illustrations, 2s. 6d.

Barefooted Birdie.
A SIMPLE TALE.
By T. O'T.,
Edited by CHARLES FELIX, Author of "Velvet Lawn," &c.

"We cannot recommend a better present than 'Barefooted Birdie,' a simple tale for Christmas."—*John Bull.*

"We can give this tale our very highest praise."—*Church Review.*

"The whole story is like a gleam of bright sunshine and summer weather just stealing in upon the cold fogs and winds of Christmas, and telling of brighter days to come in spring and summer, and of brighter seasons still in the far-off golden land, where 'they need no candle nor light of the sun,' to which 'Birdie' and her little brother Steevie won their happy way."—*Standard.*

"It is a story such as all little people who rejoice in a book at the chimney corner will find just to their heart's content, and in which older and graver readers will find many a touch of true poetry and pathos. 'Birdie' will be read by many, and must please all who are worth pleasing and care to be pleased. We have had nothing so good since Andersen's 'Little Match Girl,' of whom 'Birdie' reminds us."—*Herald.*

"Full of true, hearty, Christian feeling, thoroughly sound and healthy in tone, and altogether a book which we can most cordially recommend."—*Church & State Rev.*

In 1 vol. post 8vo, bevelled edges, 6s., cloth.

The Staff Surgeon;
Or, LIFE IN ENGLAND AND CANADA.
A Story. By E. S. T.

"A pretty, interesting story, pleasantly told, and distinguished by a quiet grace. It is in another sense a charming book, delightful to look at, to read or to touch."—*Court Circular.*

"The tale is fluently written, and contains some pleasant descriptive passages."—*Dispatch.*

"Pleasantly and genially written; and scattered through various parts of the narrative are to be found some truthful and life-like descriptions of scenes both in this country and in Canada."—*Observer.*

"A thoroughly readable novel. The story is highly interesting, and some of the characters exceedingly well drawn."—*Star.*

In 1 vol. small 8vo, 3s. 6d.

Life's Paths.
A TALE OF OUR OWN DAY.
By the Author of "Gentle Influence," "Amy's Trials," &c.
With Frontispiece.

"We seldom remember coming across a story with less "sensation" in it, and yet so really interesting. Some very valuable lessons are taught in an eminently natural manner. The different characters are very well drawn. We suspect several are studies from real life."—*Church Review.*

"'Life's Paths' may be safely recommended, and that which it professes to aim at it successfully works out, and that is no slight thing to say of any book in these days."—*Churchman.*

"A well intentioned, conscientiously written book, wherein it is impossible to find anything objectionable."—*Mrng. Post.*

"The tale is pleasing and refined."—*Globe.*

In 1 vol. post 8vo, elegantly bound, 7s. 6d.

Tales at the Outspan;

Or, Adventures in the Wild Regions of Southern Africa.
By CAPTAIN A. W. DRAYSON,
Author of "Sporting Scenes in South Africa, &c.
New and Cheaper Edition,
Illustrated with numerous Woodcuts.

"To read about adventures with wild beasts is always pleasant; in fact, there is an idea in the youthful mind that lions and tigers were created specially to furnish material for exciting stories, and in very truth Captain Drayson gives us adventure enough and tells us as much in one volume as we have a right to look for, about lions and leopards, elephants and buffaloes, not to speak of those more savage animals called Kaffirs."—*Herald*.

"'Tales at the Outspan' will be found an admirable Gift Book.—The binding is so rich, the illustrations are so very good, and above all the tales are so enthralling, that every reader, be he man or boy, will delight in the volume."—*Standard*.

"We are happy to see that this volume has reached a second edition. It is a boy's book of the very best kind, a book of adventure, peril, and excitement, pervaded by a most healthful flavour of exertion, and enterprise, and self denial."—*Spectator*.

"Among the most pleasant books that have been written on South African adventure is this by Captain Drayson, inasmuch as it is not a mere record of wild beast butchery, but describes stirring combats with these by no means contemptible foes, and the savage native tribes."—*Dispatch*.

In 1 vol., post 8vo, 10s. 6d.

Tangles and Tales.

Being the RECORD OF A TWELVEMONTH'S IMBROGLIO.
By E. C. MOGRIDGE.

"We have shown that Mr. Mogridge knows how to tell a good story cleverly."—*John Bull*.

"Written in a light and pleasant style. Some of the tales have a romantic, others somewhat of a tragic interest, and a fair proportion of them have incidents of love and mystery very gracefully interwoven in the narrative."—*Observer*.

"Mr. Mogridge possesses all the talent necessary to eliminate a plot, with not a little aptness of description, no small power of observation, and a real sense of humour, as his volume sufficiently proves."—*Literary Gazette*.

"It is highly to be praised for the healthy tone it manifests."—*Bell's Messenger*.

"This pleasant volume of 'Tales' is by Mr. Mogridge, a son of 'Old Humphrey,' whose useful and simple duodecimo volumes are so common in the pack of the Diocesan book-hawker, and are so appreciated by the purchasers from it * * * Some of these tales are of far more than average merit, and they are all of them very readable; and any one who wants a chatty, soothing story-book cannot do better than invest in 'Tangles and Tales.'"—*Churchman*.

"As the scene of several is laid in foreign parts, a reasonable variety is secured to the characters and their surroundings."—*London Review*.

"The writer possesses no slight powers of observation, and his descriptive passages give to the mind something of the same effect as the sight of a carefully-drawn picture. We have derived great pleasure from the perusal of 'Tangles and Tales.'"—*Public Opinion*.

POETRY.

In 1 vol. post 8vo., 10s. 6d. Third edition, revised.
The Greek Pastoral Poets.
Translated and Edited by Dr. M. J. CHAPMAN.

In 1 vol. post 8vo., 10s. 6d.
Hebrew Idylls and Dramas.
By Dr. M. J. CHAPMAN.
Originally published in " Frazer's Magazine."

In 1 vol. Foolscap 8vo., 3s 6d.
Jersey Legends;
In VERSE.
By THOMAS WILLIAMS.

In 1 vol. post 8vo, bevelled edges, 6s.
Arno's Waters;
AND OTHER POEMS.
By FRANCES JANE FORSAYTH.

In Foolscap 8vo, 2s. 6d.
The Alchymist:
PARABLES IN RHYME.
By Capt. C. N. TUCKER, late Bengal Cavalry.

"Much above the average of little books of this class, for it is free from gross faults of any kind."—*Spectator.*

RECENTLY PUBLISHED.

ARNOLD—THE MARQUESS OF DALHOUSIE'S ADMINISTRATION OF BRITISH INDIA.
By EDWIN ARNOLD, M.A., late Principal of Poona College, and Fellow of the University of Bombay. Vol. I., containing the Acquisition and Administration of the Punjab. 8vo, 15s.

BROMLEY—A WOMAN'S WANDERINGS IN THE WESTERN WORLD.
A Series of Letters addressed to Sir Fitzroy Kelly, M.P. By his Daughter, Mrs. BROMLEY. 1 vol., post 8vo, with Illustrations, 10s. 6d.

DENISON—REMARKS ON ESSAYS AND REVIEWS.
By Sir WILLIAM DENISON, K.C.B., F.R.S., F.A.S., Colonel Royal Engineers. 8vo, 1s. 6d.

FAITH AND PEACE,
Being Answers to Essays and Reviews. By Several Writers, with a Preface by the Venerable Archdeacon Denison. 1 vol., 8vo, 12s.

FONBLANQUE—NIPHON AND PE-CHE-LI;
Or, Two Years in Japan and Northern China. By EDWARD BARRINGTON DE FONBLANQUE, Assistant Commissary-General. 1 vol. 8vo. with Illustrations, 21s.

GODKIN—EDUCATION IN IRELAND.
Its History, Institutions, Systems, Statistics, and Progress, from the Earliest Times to the Present. By JAMES GODKIN. 8vo, 7s. 6d.

HANDBOOK OF TURNING,
Containing Instructions in Concentric, Elliptic, and Eccentric Turning; also various Plates of Chucks, Tools, &c., and a Portrait of the author done in the Lathe. A New Edition, fcp. 8vo, 7s. 6d.

HARTLEY—A HANDY BOOK FOR RIFLE VOLUNTEERS;
or, a Compendium of Instruction for Drill and the Rifle, according to the most Recent Regulations. Arranged systematically and specially adapted to the Progressive Improvement of the Volunteer in Every Stage. By Captain W. G. HARTLEY. 1 vol., fcap. 8vo, 7s 6d.

HUGHES—BIBLIOLATRY, AN ESSAY.
By the Rev. JAMES HUGHES, M.A. 1 vol., fcap. 8vo, 2s. 6d.

JOYCE—ECCLESIA VINDICATA,
A Treatise on Appeals in Matters Spiritual. By JAMES MAYLAND JOYCE, M.A., author of a "Constitutional History of the Convocation of the Clergy," &c. 1 vol., fcp. 8vo, 5s. 6d.

LANGUAGE OF FLOWERS,
With Illustrative Poetry; to which are now added the Calendar of Flowers, and the Dial of Flowers. Thirteenth edition, 1 vol., fcp. 8vo, with coloured Plates, 7s. 6d.

LAURIE—NORTHERN EUROPE
(Denmark, Sweden, Russia), Local, Social, and Political. By Captain W. F. B. LAURIE, late Commissary of Ordnance, Nagpore Force. 1 vol., 8vo.

LECTURES ON THE MOUNTAINS;
Or, the Highlands and Highlanders as they were and as they are. 2 vols., fcap. 8vo, 10s.

LEE—ON MIRACLES.
An Examination of the Remarks "On the Study of the Evidences of Christianity," in "Essays and Reviews." By WILLIAM LEE, D.D. 1 vol., 8vo, 5s.

MACKAY—THE GOUTY PHILOSOPHER;
Or, the Opinions, Whims, and Eccentricities of John Wagstaffe, Esq., of Wilbye Grange. By CHAS. MACKAY. 1 vol., post 8vo, 10s. 6d.

NEALE—ESSAYS ON LITURGIOLOGY AND
CHURCH HISTORY. By the Rev. J. M. NEALE, D.D. 1 vol., 8vo, 18s.

NORTHCOTE—TWENTY YEARS OF FI-
NANCIAL POLICY. A Summary of the Chief Financial Measures passed between 1842 and 1861, with a Table of Budgets. By Sir STAFFORD H. NORTHCOTE, Bart., M.P., 1 vol., 8vo, 14s.

ONGARA—BARON RICASOLI,
Prime Minister of Italy. A Biography. From the Italian of F. DALL' ONGARA. 1 vol., fcap. 8vo, 3s. 6d.

PERRY—THE HISTORY OF THE CHURCH
OF ENGLAND FROM THE DEATH OF ELIZABETH TO THE PRESENT TIME. By the Rev. G. G. PERRY, M.A. In 3 vols., 8vo, price 21s. each.

RECOLLECTIONS of GENERAL GARIBALDI;
Or, Travels from Rome to Lucerne, comprising a Visit to the Mediterranean, Isles of La Maddelena and Caprera, and General Garibaldi's Home. 1 vol., post 8vo, 10s. 6d.

MATILDA OF NORMANDY,
A Poetical Tribute to the Imperial Academy of Caen. By H. M. CAREY. 2s.

NUPTIALS OF BARCELONA,
A Tale of Priestly Frailty and Spanish Tyranny.

POEMS.
By the Author of "Paul Ferroll." Including a New Edition of IX Poems by V. 1 vol., fcp. 8vo, 7s. 6d.

PARISH HYMN BOOK.
Edited by the Rev. H. W. Beadon, the Rev. Greville Phillimore, and the Rev. James Russell Woodford. Price 8d. and 1s.

RECOLLECTIONS OF THE PAST. 3s. 6d.

SACRED POEMS.
By the late Right Hon. Sir ROBERT GRANT, a New Edition, with a Notice by Lord Glenelg. 5s.

SATAN RESTORED.
By W. CYPLES. 6s.

SHADOW OF THE YEW.
By NORMAN B. YONGE.

STILL SMALL VOICE.
A Poem in Four Cantos. By NORMAN B. YONGE. 6s. 6d.

SUMMER SONGS.
By MORTIMER COLLINS. 3s. 6d.

www.ingramcontent.com/pod-product-compliance
Lightning Source LLC
Chambersburg PA
CBHW030245170426
43202CB00009B/628